CW00521093

Money I

– A Historical Journey

Emil Sandstedt

Table of Contents

Preface

This is not a history book, nor a book on anthropology. Neither is it a book on economics or on numismatics specifically. Instead, it uses all these sciences in order to arrive at more general conclusions regarding the nature and properties of *money*. The subject of money is in some ways more complicated than it appears, and, in other ways simpler as well. Perhaps anthropologist Alison Hingston Quiggin got it right when she stated that "everyone, except an economist, knows what 'money' means"[1]. Be that as it may, it is because of this confusion that much is written and said about money that does not hold up well in the face of logical frameworks, or historical evidence. With this book I hope to make money easier to understand and show how most monies that once reigned for decades or even centuries, now are sure to be long vanished.

The part of the book on primitive monies draws from Paul Einzig's *Primitive Money – In its Ethnological, Historical and Economic Aspects*, which was the first ever volume of substantial size fully devoted to the subject. Einzig wrote it in the shadow of World War II with a desire to "escape from the horrors of the present into the remote past"[2]. It would be not just a bit much for me to claim similar motivations, but it should be noted that this book is written in the shadow of unabashed physical and digital money production, and of a lack of discourse with regards to the deleterious economic and social effects of such activities. The book also draws from Alison Hingston Quiggin's *A Survey of*

---

[1] (Quiggin, 1949, p. 1)
[2] (Einzig, 1949, p. v)

Primitive Money, and intertwines much of Einzig's and Hingston Quiggin's findings with various historical accounts in order to arrive at conclusions on the nature and properties of money. More specifically, the conclusions concern the *hard-* and *easy money* framework pioneered through the brief *stock-to-flow* discussions in Antal Fekete's article *Whither Gold?*[3], and which was further developed and popularized by Saifedean Ammous in *The Bitcoin Standard*[4]. *Money Dethroned*, incorporating also the debasement of metallic monies into this framework, provides a similar but complementary Mengerian[5] understanding of the nature and properties of money, through further historical observations.

Einzig, in the preface to his revised edition, brought up criticism to the approach of drawing conclusions from broad studies. Certain contemporaries argued that by having failed to concentrate on gathering first-hand knowledge of one single area, society or tribe, Einzig's "unfashionable" method of covering hundreds of anthropological examples had inherent weaknesses. I am of the opinion that, when dealing with money, a broad approach is essential given the global nature of the phenomenon. If the focus is narrowed down, either spatially or temporally, a student of monies might be exposed to idiosyncratic conditions not always relevant for a more complete understanding. As, for example, evidence of isolated cases of seashell money were found on multiple continents, it clearly tells us that the attempts toward advancing crude barter have taken many curious, but – and this is important – non-random roads. So it may be wise, in a proverbial sense, to travel all of these in order to understand the dynamics of the emergence and the dethronement of money.

---

[3] See (Fekete, 1996), specifically the section "The role of plunder".

[4] (Ammous, 2018)

[5] See (Menger, Principles of Economics, 1871), Chapter VIII.

As for the historical first-hand accounts in the book, they come in the form of often translated historical writings. The validity and consistency of such documents vary of course, but for the purpose of this book they are adequately contributing to the understanding we seek. I figured it an exciting narrative to let the reader follow in the footsteps of one of these sources – Shaykh Abú 'Abdalláh Muhammad ibn Battúta – a 14th century Muslim theologian and judge from Morocco, who travelled far and wide across Africa, Europe and Asia. We know of his journeys thanks to his countryman Ibn Juzayy, who put Battúta's adventures into the written word after the latter had finally returned home. The complete Arabic version of Juzayy's writings was found in Algeria only a couple of years after Samuel Lee's 1829 publication of an incomplete manuscript. It was translated first to French by Defrémery and Sanguinetti, and then again from Arabic to highly understandable English by H.A.R. Gibb in the beginning of the 20th century. These translations quickly spread to a fascinated Western audience, and I am happy to at least partly contribute to the revival of an interest in them.

Emil Sandstedt

A Short Introduction to Money

The Origin Story

In H.A.R Gibb's 1929 translation of Ibn Battúta's travel records, the translator starts the valuable compendium with a recognition that every passing day, over time, becomes part of history:

> To the world of today the men of medieval Christendom already seem remote and unfamiliar. Their names and deeds are recorded in our history books, their monuments still adorn our cities, but our kinship with them is a thing unreal, which costs an effort of the imagination. (Battúta, 1325-1354, p. 1)

The same, I would argue, can more or less be said about money. We read and hear about money used in the past, and we judge various examples as strange, or backward. But only by studying monies in detail can we understand what they meant for the people who worked hard to accumulate them, and it is possible that we leave the studies with, at a minimum, a slightly higher dose of humility and a little bit less of ridicule. Mongol tribes that used livestock as money were serious about it; they had this type of money because it was judged by individuals a superior way to carry wealth and facilitate current and future economic exchange. Tribes of modern day Tanzania strived toward similar goals by using colorful glass beads as money.

The longer one were to look at monetary systems of the past, the more fascinating types of primitive monies are sure to be found. This inadvertently raises questions. How did such monies first emerge and who chose which medium to use for that purpose? How come various societies, tribes or nations used different monies and why did they not all use one single money in order to make trade across these places easier? For answers to these questions, we have to overlook Quiggin's tongue-in-cheek remark about economists and turn to *On the Origins of Money* by Carl Menger – a 19th century writer who can be considered the father of the Austrian School of Economics.

Menger starts his explanation of the emergence of money in the following way:

> *There is a phenomenon which has from of old and in a peculiar degree attracted the attention of social philosophers and practical economists, the fact of certain commodities (these being in advanced civilizations coined pieces of gold and silver, together subsequently with documents representing those coins) becoming universally acceptable media of exchange. […]*
>
> *It must not be supposed that the form of coin, or document, employed as current-money, constitutes the enigma in this phenomenon. We may look away from these forms and go back to earlier stages of economic development, or indeed to what still obtains in countries here and there, where we find the precious metals in a uncoined state serving as the medium of exchange, and even certain other commodities, cattle, skins, cubes of tea, slabs of salt, cowrie-shells, etc.; still we are*

> *confronted by this phenomenon, still we have to*
> *explain why it is that the economic man is ready*
> *to accept a certain kind of commodity, even if he*
> *does not need it, or if his need of it is already*
> *supplied, in exchange for all the goods he has*
> *brought to market [...]. (Menger, On the Origins*
> *of Money, 1892, pp. 11-12)*

Understanding Menger's initial point about individuals accepting commodities they don't need is crucial. The explanation can be found in the core problem that money solves: *the double coincidence of wants*. While initially sounding complicated, it is not. Let us imagine a valley, occupied by a number of farmsteads. As barter initially is extremely limited between the individual farms in the valley, each farmer has to grow and produce a number of goods, because one specific good alone is not nearly enough for each of them to survive and thrive. The reality of this initial limitation of economic exchange, in other words, results in each farmer growing and producing goods like cows, potatoes, wheat, apples, firewood etc.

Now, it may be that a farmer in one especially sunny part of the valley grows such a large quantity of apples that he and his family neither could, nor want to eat them all, or even a majority of them. It may therefore be the case that the farmer finds more of his needs and wants satisfied than before, should he be able to find exchange opportunities with neighbors producing goods he himself has a hard time producing, like firewood for instance. His goal, therefore, is finding other individuals in want of his surplus apples and whom are also willing to give up their surpluses of firewood.

Let us now imagine that the farmer, while expanding his barter network, walks to a forested part of the valley, to a hut owned by a firewood producer. Upon reaching her, it might be the case that she, while having an abundance of firewood collected, does not need or want apples in exchange. It might be the case that she wants pears, wheat, or cows, or any other good that the apple farmer, to his disappointment, currently does not produce much of. This is the lack of a *double coincidence of wants*; for an economic exchange to occur, which satisfies both him and her in this case, she must have the type of good, and quantity, that he wants, and he must have the type of good, and quantity, that she wants. Since he does not have pears, nor enough wheat or cows, no economic exchange can occur and he has to try with other firewood producers. This type of problem has historically been observed, for example in 19th century Borneo by Hugh Brooke Low:

> *[...] a Dyak has no conception of the use of a circulating medium. He may be seen wandering in the Bazaar with a ball of beeswax in his hand for days together, because he can't find anybody willing to take it for the exact article he requires.* (Roth, 1896, p. 231)

Imagine now that the apple farmer, before embarking on further exchange missions, gathers some information, not only on which firewood producers are demanding apples, but also on which goods of the valley, in general, are sought after by a multitude of bartering individuals. It may be the case that only two out of a dozen firewood producers accept apples at this time, and only one of them could perhaps supply him with the amount of firewood he wants for his surplus of apples. Unless he finds an *intermediary good* accepted in barter by more firewood producers, he will in practice only have one exchange opportunity, which might cause him to have to accept a suboptimal exchange rate as his stored surplus of apples would start to rot over time. Menger muses on this problem as well:

> *Consider how seldom it is the case, that a commodity owned by somebody is of less value in use than another commodity owned by somebody*

else! And for the latter just the opposite relation is the case. But how much more seldom does it happen that these two bodies meet! Think, indeed, of the peculiar difficulties obstructing the immediate barter of goods in those cases, where supply and demand do not quantitatively coincide; where, e.g., an indivisible commodity is to be exchanged for a variety of goods in the possession of different person, or indeed for such commodities as are only in demand at different times and can be supplied only by different persons! (Menger, On the Origins of Money, 1892, pp. 19-20)

In other words, it may be in this apple farmer's economic interest to seek out, for example, wheat farmers, whose produce are demanded by a considerable number of firewood producers. And so, while the apple farmer perhaps has no intention of ever consuming any of the wheat that he goes to barter for, it may be the case that a number of wheat farmers are in want of his apples, and so can give him better exchange terms than what the firewood producer would have. After having exchanged his apples to bags of wheat, he suddenly has, not one, but a number of barter opportunities with the firewood producers. When the nature of direct barter imposes barriers on his exchange opportunities in the valley, it is very likely to his economic benefit to circumvent those barriers through *indirect barter*, meaning the acquisition of an intermediary good that, at the time, is a better medium of exchange due to its broad acceptance.

As the apple farmer is not the only individual in the valley trying to exchange his own produce for other goods, it logically follows that the good in the valley with a relatively high grade of acceptance in barter – or *saleableness* – gradually has its saleableness enhanced even further as individuals like our farmer use it as a medium of exchange. Because it must be

14

remembered that also the firewood producers, and many others, will look for an intermediary good in order to circumvent the same costly problem. Menger has the following to say about the relationship between saleableness and money:

> *These difficulties [lack of coincident of wants] would have proved absolutely insurmountable obstacles to the progress of traffic, and at the same time to the production of goods not commanding a regular sale, had there not lain a remedy in the very nature of things, to wit, the different degrees of saleableness (Absatzfähigkeit) of commodities. [...]*
>
> *The theory of money necessarily presupposes a theory of the saleableness of goods. If we grasp this, we shall be able to understand how the almost unlimited saleableness of money is only a special case, — presenting only a difference of degree — of a generic phenomenon of economic life — namely, the difference in the saleableness of commodities in general. (Menger, On the Origins of Money, 1892, pp. 20-21)*

With the progression of barter, meaning also the indirect barter as described above, it naturally leads to conveniently situated marketplaces forming so that the resources spent on travelling between farmsteads or villages decrease substantially. In these marketplaces, it is easy to imagine both barter exchanges as well as indirect barter exchanges (perhaps with multiple media of exchange initially[6]), occurring for quite some time in parallel. But as the most saleable intermediary good gradually accrues ever higher saleableness due to individuals cost-minimizing their

---

[6] Einzig presents evidence of parallel grain- and silver money, in the Babylonian Code of Hammurabi (Einzig, 1949, p. 213).

economic actions, it is also ever more economical for those who still barter directly, or still barter indirectly with a less saleable intermediary good, to instead barter indirectly only with the most saleable intermediary good. Menger sums up the dynamic coherently:

> *Men have been led, with increasing knowledge of their individual interests, each by his own economic interests, without convention, without legal compulsion, nay, even without any regard to the common interest, to exchange goods destined for exchange (their "wares") for other goods equally destined for exchange, but more saleable. (Menger, On the Origins of Money, 1892, p. 34)*

The most saleable good in the valley (and more specifically in its marketplaces) is what is called *money*. In fact, there is a large body of etymological evidence, which we will return to later, pointing to the fact that the very words for "money", often were indistinguishable from words for various traded goods, like cowries or livestock. The specific money good in the valley is now demanded not only for the uses it had prior to becoming money, but also for the specific use case of facilitating much more efficient barter, or economic exchange, now as well as in the future. Phrased slightly differently, money is the best interspatial, intertemporal and interscalable medium of exchange. Menger:

> *When the relatively most saleable commodities have become "money," the great event has in the first place the effect of substantially increasing their originally high saleableness. Every economic subject bringing less saleable wares to market, to acquire goods of another sort, has thenceforth a stronger interest in converting what he has in the first instance into the wares which have become*

money. [...] (Menger, On the Origins of Money, 1892, p. 39)

Thus the effect produced by such goods as are relatively most saleable becoming money is an increasing differentiation between their degree of saleableness and that of all other goods. And this difference in saleableness ceases to be altogether gradual, and must be regarded in a certain aspect as something absolute. (Menger, On the Origins of Money, 1892, pp. 42-43)

Saleableness Besieged

It is important to understand that the origin story of a good emerging as money does not necessarily end with the good's now more or less absolute state of superior saleableness. We can easily imagine how bags of wheat emerged as money in the valley discussed earlier (this happened historically in various Indian societies)[7]. And for a long time it can perhaps function well as highly liquid, divisible and uniform money. But the saleableness of a good is affected by many factors. As the society of the valley progresses into ever higher degrees of civilization, it may turn out that wheat money has certain disadvantages at these later stages. Since the valley produces ever more goods and ever more surpluses, it might prove difficult to store the wheat money over long time periods as it naturally starts to decay if in contact with damp air. The saleableness across time, once not really a problem, may now be found to be lacking enough for individuals around the valleys to act. While having once fully shouldered the mantle of money, wheat may end up losing it in favor of another good now better suited, like small, useful iron rods that do not very well decay to the same degree. Such parallel instances of money have been very common across the world precisely because they solved for different and shifting considerations of saleableness. One medium, like wheat, was used in smaller transactions and as petty change, while the other medium, like iron rods, was used in larger transactions.

The loss in relative saleableness of wheat, if severe enough, can even lead to a full new iteration of a single good emerging as money. In other words, wheat may in our example slowly be demonetized in favor of more durable iron rod money. Menger emphasizes that these iterations are not exactly coordinated, but

---

[7] (Einzig, 1949, pp. 113-114)

the result of individuals trying to minimize various incurred costs (in this case related to deterioration, or rot):

> It is obvious how highly significant a factor is habit in the genesis of such generally serviceable means of exchange. It lies in the economic interest of each trafficking individual to exchange less saleable for more saleable commodities. But the willing acceptance of the medium of exchange presupposes already a knowledge of these interest on the part of those economic subjects who are expected to accept in exchange for their wares a commodity which in and by itself is perhaps entirely useless to them. It is certain that this knowledge never arises in every part of a nation at the same time. It is only in the first instance a limited number of economic subjects who will recognize the advantage in such procedure, an advantage which, in and by itself, is independent of the general recognition of a commodity as a medium of exchange, inasmuch as such an exchange, always and under all circumstances, brings the economic unit a good deal nearer to his goal, to the acquisition of useful things of which he really stands in need. (Menger, On the Origins of Money, 1892, p. 36)

As trade with other valleys and villages develops, where sometimes identical monetary systems emerged, and sometimes not, the cost for traders to transport iron rods might be an ever higher inconvenience due to the general low valuation per weight unit. The saleableness across space, in other words, may this time be found to be lacking. This is not at all a hypothetical problem, but has been observed historically. In Belgian Congo, Europeans found themselves having to deal with such iron money, "which was apt to reduce itself to absurdity because of the disproportionate high cost of transport"[8]. It is easy to imagine a gradual shift from iron money to, for example, copper – a metal almost always valued higher per weight unit.

The dynamic described above, of that of monies naturally getting dethroned in favor of goods better suited, has historically shown itself countless times. One good example comes from nomadic populations that used livestock as money while roaming the steppes and grasslands. As they became ever more sedentary and built growing towns, the costs of storing their livestock money at home obviously became ever more burdensome due to a general lack of space. This created a pressure on the saleableness of that money, which ultimately had it dethroned in favor of, among other things, copper, silver, and gold. Traces of such a development in the form of animal depictions were prevalent in early coinage.[9] Etymology provides rich examples as well, where for example the Old Germanic word for livestock, *fehu*, today exists as the English "fee"[10].

One could now imagine that the dynamics of these iterations are more or less understood. But there is still one important external factor affecting the saleableness of money, which we have not yet considered. It is the dilution- and debasement resistance of the money. It may very well be the case that a money, while having emerged after a number of iterations, and while having properties that cause it to be highly transportable, durable, divisible, fungible, and so on, still sees its saleableness suffer due to being easily produced, or more specifically, diluted.

The root of this problem stems from what happens to the valuation of a good once its monetization process has started. Aside from having an ever higher saleableness in relation to the other goods – a dynamic which we saw ended as something near

---

[8] (Einzig, 1949, p. 161)

[9] (Menger, Principles of Economics, 1871, pp. 266-267)

[10] (Einzig, 1949, p. 259)

absolute – it is always the case that the valuation of said good increases as well. Prior to monetization, the good was subjectively valued by individuals only for its original use cases, but now it is suddenly valued for the vital use case of facilitating the cheapest possible barter, or economic exchange. In a society of surpluses, it facilitates savings, which is just another word for deferred economic exchange. It turns out that this use case is important enough to individuals for them to value the monetary good high above its ordinary use value. An excellent example of this is gold which, although used in industries, is valued by individuals mostly for its good monetary properties and consequent high saleableness.

It must further be understood that the monetary good in question was collected or produced by individuals also before it emerged as money. Seeing an increase in its demand and consequently its valuation in comparison to all, or at least most, other goods, this of course acts as information to the collectors or the producers, signaling that it is suddenly profitable to expend more resources in order to acquire more units. In other words, any good being monetized quickly attracts more production, meaning higher dilution of the existing supply, meaning a dampening effect on the price. For holders of this money then, this additional factor has to be accounted for when considering future saleableness. If we return to the example of the valley, it may have been the case that the demonetization of iron rods and the monetization of copper rods certainly solved for costs related to both transportability and durability, but the now relatively high valuation of copper may have set in motion enough added annual production of new copper units, in this valley and others, that individuals using such rods as money suddenly find themselves having to bear this additional cost as well. It is in their economic interest therefore, should they need to use much money over a short time period, or even little money over a long time period, to seek out goods with higher resistance to such dilution, yet with similar monetary properties with regards to saleableness across scale, space and time.

Perhaps it is now clear, that the next iterations of a good getting monetized ought to occur for metals that were even harder to dilute than copper, like silver or gold. It is natural for individuals to want to escape this cost, and so the very same broader dynamic of cost minimization with regards to economic exchange, that dethroned wheat in favor of iron, and iron in favor of copper, now makes itself known again. Individuals holding money over a non-negligible period of time is in a constant and losing battle with the producers of said money, and it is often in their self-interest to apply some time and resources in trying to figure out how to escape this dilution, perhaps not with all of their current money, but with a part of it.

In a step to quantify and emphasize monetary dilution, Antal Fekete came up with the *stock-to-flow* ratio. The stock is the current supply of a good, while the flow is the estimated upcoming production, often arbitrarily limited to the upcoming year. It is, in other words, the inverted monetary inflation, causing it to be tautological in some sense. But for an example of how it is actually used, let us look at silver and gold. Silver has a rather large stock, but due to the relative ease with which this metal is produced, the annual flow is high in relation to it. The stock-to-flow of silver then, may in our hypothetical example be 5, meaning a 20% annual dilution. Gold, having been accumulated and hoarded for millennia while not being easily destroyed, also has a rather large stock, albeit smaller than silver's. Yet, since gold is extremely hard to extract from the ground, the annual flow is small, much more so that silver's. This causes gold to have a high stock-to-flow ratio – often higher than 50, which directly implies around 2% annual dilution.

Now, is this quantitative measurement enough for a cost-minimizing individual to speculate on which medium to choose as the best facilitator of economic exchange? Not really, according to Saifedean Ammous[11]. To go further in estimating resistance to dilution, individuals have to judge and estimate the effect of an increase in valuation of, in this case, silver and gold, on future production of the money. It is already established that the monetization process of a good leads to it being higher valued, which signals to producers to produce more units of it. By thinking in terms of such resistance to dilution in the face of increased valuation – a property known as *hardness* – individuals can try to predict costs currently unseen. Ben Kaufman defines hardness in the following way:

> *The hardness of money is in reverse relation to the monetary inflation, and the consequent dilution of the value of the existing stock, which can economically be inflicted on it. (Kaufman, 2019)*

From history, we know that even in periods of high gold valuation, the annual production, or flow, remained limited due to gold's relatively scarce state in nature. In periods of high silver valuation, however, the annual production had room to expand considerably due to silver's relatively abundant state in nature. Under such a scenario, gold's stock-to-flow ratio would be little disturbed, while silver's stock-to-flow ratio would deteriorate substantially.

The concept of hardness, along with other factors, help explain why gold in the end emerged as money, first in many societies all over the world, and finally more or less everywhere, including in our hypothetical valley of farmsteads. With this in mind, it is soon time to embark on Ibn Battúta's journey to verify these claims. Are the dynamics of money properly described? It is up to the reader to decide after observing the many accounts by the travelers. And, it should finally be added, the written

---

[11] See (Ammous, 2018), Chapter 3.

accounts themselves were never made to prove any point with regards to this matter; neither the theologian Battúta, nor his Christian counterparts, cared much for money as an economic phenomenon. We can thus trust that they described the situations at hand in a neutral way.

Misconceptions

Finally, for our understanding of money, a couple of more topics ought to be briefly discussed. It has recently been the case that prominent authors of various disciplines describe money as purely a phenomenon of collective coordination, or legislation, rather than emerging naturally out of pragmatic cost considerations by individuals as described in this book. Money, they have argued, is a "social construct", or a "shared illusion", or something even more mystical. Shades of such a notion is seen even in the word "money", which is derived from Latin *moneta* – a goddess in whose Roman temple money was coined (Quiggin, 1949, p. 271). To the detriment of the public's understanding of money, some economists have even tried to use different shades of this mysticism in order to appear intellectual and forward thinking, to argue for collective control over money, or to even attempt the introduction of their own bastardized versions of it. Needless to say, while it may sound emotionally compelling to some, money is just as little a shared illusion as is a regular marketplace or bazaar, which will become more apparent with the next chapters in this book. Infusing it with mysticism only muddles economic discourse.

Perhaps slightly less vague but more urgent to address, is the claim by some people – often politicians in need of taxes – that money is indeed something so mystical that it acquires close to magical properties. An artificial increase in the production of money, they argue, rather than just causing prices to increase, spurs the economy as more hoarded money is spent and enters "into circulation". By effortlessly creating more money, a situation develops similar to that of a casino where the house can suddenly force its customers to hit its bar or roulette wheels. This misconception, that inflation spurs growth, always fails to reconcile the disconnect in how, on the one hand, enforcing uneconomic exchange between individuals can, on the other hand, be good for "society", or "the people", or any other vague term conjured up to represent what is just a collection of exactly such individuals. The aftermath of such authoritarian thinking was observed by Ibn Battúta in India, as we shall see.

Another misconception about money is that by circumventing the laborious process of, for example, digging up precious metals, a society lowers the total cost of the monetary system. It is true that from a certain perspective, the digging of giant holes, tunnels and pits, for ore later processed and struck into coinage, may perhaps be seen as a highly wasteful venture. What people tend to forget about easily produced money, however, is the hidden costs that from time to time appear and inadvertently suffocate trade and production. Since the cost of money production is low, mass production is suddenly economical, creating a situation where such innovative and modern monetary systems were indeed saved from the frying pan, just to be chaotically put into the fire instead. The sudden low cost of money production has time and time again thrown economies into states of incredibly high and destructive monetary inflation, with accompanying deterioration of trade, of savings, and in the end, of dignity as the authorities overstep their bounds in clumsy attempts to counter the ever more grim situation. Ibn Battúta observed the early stage of precisely such a monetary system in the Yuan dynasty's China. Two other early examples of where the cost argument for easily produced money and against specie led to first the implementation and then the implosion of paper money, were the scheme of John Law, and the Assignat experiment. Unlike laborious silver or gold, the efficient, effortless paper quickly propelled the people of France into abject poverty, starvation, or guillotines.

With all this said, it is instead with Menger's rather sober description of money that we with clarity can understand that it is not mystical or magical, but just the most saleable good of indirect barter. Money, fulfilling such an incredibly important role for the prospering of individuals, is therefore nothing to be tampered or experimented with. It is, on the contrary, the result of a conscious effort on the part of individuals, and should be left to their discretion just as any other market activity.

Vol I: Primitive Money

While referred to as "primitive", monies such as cowries and glass beads were inherently not much different from the more modern metallic monetary systems. It is a classification of such arbitrary political convenience that John Maynard Keynes saw it fit to throw even gold in there:

> *In truth, the gold standard is already a barbarous relic. [...] Advocates of the ancient standard do not observe how remote it now is from the spirit and the requirements of the age. (Keynes, 1924, pp. 172-173)*

With the same logic, modern digitized paper money may be claimed to be no less primitive than its monetary predecessors. In fact, owing to the state of utter backwardness that paper money societies so often have been catapulted back to, it is perhaps more fitting than not to include Battúta's observation of the illustrious Kublai Khan's senseless tree bark money in this part of the book as well. Other curious but better forms of non-metallic money Battúta directly observed and mentioned were, among others, salt, cotton cloths, furs and skins.

One property that often distinguished primitive monies from their metallic counterparts were their initial high use-value. Livestock, skins, salt etc. obviously had a great many uses to people. Such goods kept them fed, warm and healthy. A considerable use-value therefore worked in tandem with their exchange-value. This could be both to their advantage and disadvantage, as while saleableness often increased with use-value, consumption of such goods also decreased the total stock, meaning the stock-to-flow ratio became more vulnerable to disruption.

As we have already touched upon during the introduction to money, primitive monies often lacked certain monetary properties that later coinage did not. Monetary units were not always fungible, which must have become apparent for Mongols using sheep as money. A young, healthy sheep likely fetched a different price than an old one. Some monies deteriorated over time, like bags of grain or iron. Other monies were not easily transportable, like the famous Rai stones in the Pacific Ocean. Any attempt to divide some of the above monies could obviously be tricky as well, which sometimes made circumventing the double coincidence of wants hard.

Unlike their metallic counterparts, primitive monies often lacked official stamping of various sorts. They were because of this usually easier to legally produce and dilute through private ventures. Though the main disadvantage with many of these monies in the end were their lack of monetary hardness, they did in many cases lack the very centralized control that, as we shall see later, often was a main cause for recurring and oppressive debasements of metallic monies. It happened that certain rulers broke the very laws of arithmetic in order to debase primitive money in a roundabout way, as was the case in Dahomey where a string of 1500 seashells counted as 2000 when in the hands of the king (Einzig, 1949, p. 157). Such creativity was generally the exception, however, and not the rule. This anti-tampering advantage could still not save primitive monies from ultimate dethronement as the hardness of precious metals became ever more important with the progression of civilization.

1. Money of the Oceans

Our journey in the young Berber's footsteps starts in North Africa, and more specifically in Morocco, then home to his Lawata tribe as well as the regionally powerful Marinid Sultanate. In 1325 A.D., Battúta was only 21 years old as he left for his first pilgrimage to Mecca, as well as to other places holy for him, but perhaps little did he know the journey would take him to parts of the world where few of his countrymen had ever travelled before. A vast pilgrimage and trade infrastructure stretching far into Africa and Asia had been in place for centuries, which helps explain why Battúta's thirst for exploration quickly could be adequately quenched. Having teamed up with other groups of pilgrims, the journey first took them to Algiers, and then to Bijaya where Battúta got seriously sick. Pressing on anyway, he simply noted that "If God decrees my death, it shall be on the road with my face set toward Mecca." The journey continued to Constantine (not to be confused with Constantinople), from where Battúta's party set out with great haste in fear of Arab rebels.

Incidentally, one of Battúta's first mentions of money was not in reference to its nature, but rather in reference to its relation to government. A Tunisian merchant in his company had died due to the summer heat, leaving three thousand gold dinars to his heirs in Tunis. Entrusting the sum to another man in the travelling party, the money never reached his descendants as, to Battúta's apprehension, the Tunisian government got word of the event and quickly confiscated it all. This practice seems to have been everywhere common enough for Battúta to later appreciatively mention deviations from it when residing in various other parts of the world. Perhaps partly because he understood the inherent injustice in that act, he was appointed *qadi* (Islamic judge) for the pilgrimage caravan.

The eastward journey first took Battúta to Alexandria, where he observed a badly repaired Pharos Lighthouse – built by the Macedonian Ptolemaic dynasty more than a thousand years prior, and one of the Seven Wonders of the World. He then arrived at Cairo – the "mother of cities" of the Muslim world, and a city of which we will speak more of later. Following the Nile south, Battúta and his company reached the Red Sea port town 'Aydhab, only to realize that sea traffic to the Arabian Peninsula (and Mecca) was restricted due to war:

> *One-third of the city belongs to the Sultan of Egypt and two-thirds to the King of the Bejás, who is called al-Hudrubi. On reaching Aydháb we found that al-Hudrubi was engaged in warfare with the Turks [i.e. the troops of the Sultan of Egypt], that he had sunk the ships and that the Turks had fled before him. It was impossible for us to attempt the sea-crossing, so we sold the provisions that we had made ready for it, and returned to Qús with the Arabs from whom we had hired the camels. We sailed thence down the Nile (it was at the flood time) and after an eight*

31

> days' journey reached Cairo, where I stayed only
> one night, and immediately set out for Syria. This
> was in the middle of July, 1326. (Battúta, 1325-
> 1354, p. 54)

As Battúta stared out over the blue waves of the Red Sea, it is likely that he did not yet know of seashell money. To that very town, although then war-ridden, Yemenite seafarers had regularly brought goods transported from India and beyond. The stabilizing ballast of some of their dhows consisted, not of stones or sand, but of actual seashells. And so it is in 'Aydhab, these days long deserted, that Ibn Battúta's journey first intertwines with our own.

From the Maldives to Africa

What was so special about such seashells (also known as cowries – a word derived from Hindi) that they emerged as money, not only in Africa's interior, but in Asia as well? They were useless in a practical sense, as there was no possibility to eat them, warm yourself with them, or make tools out of them. But they were undoubtedly beautiful, and adding to this beauty was the fact that, for inland communities, they might very well have carried a certain mysticism, giving rise to questions regarding their blue expanses of origin. It can be argued that seashells likely were rare ornaments or artefacts before being used as money.

Although Ibn Battúta might have seen seashells in 'Aydhab or among the many bazaars in Cairo, this is nothing that he specifically mentions. It is only later when recalling his visit to the Maldives that he first mentions such (most likely of type *Monetaria moneta*[12]):

---

[12] This species still exists in the Maldives and lives in sea weeds and shallow tide pools.

> From these islands [the Maldives] there are
> exported the fish we have mentioned, coconuts,
> cloths, and cotton turbans, as well as brass
> utensils, of which they have a great many, cowrie
> shells, and qanbar. [...] The inhabitants of these
> islands use cowrie shells as money. This is an
> animal which they gather in the sea and place in
> pits, where its flesh disappears, leaving its white
> shell. They are used for buying and selling at the
> rate of four hundred thousand shells for a gold
> dinar, but they often fall in value to twelve
> hundred thousand for a dinar. They sell them in
> exchange for rice to the people of Bengal, who also
> uses them as money, as well as to the Yemenites,
> who use them instead of sand [as ballast] in their
> ships. These shells are used also by the [blacks] in
> their lands; I saw them being sold at Malli and
> Gawgaw at the rate of 1 150 for a gold dinar.
> (Battúta, 1325-1354, p. 243)

This account from Battúta is quite fascinating, and the sheer discrepancy between valuing a gold dinar at 1 200 000 shells in the Maldives, and valuing a gold dinar at 1 150 shells in the West African Empire of Mali must have had a true impact on him. It is easy to understand the motivation that caused Yemenite seafarers to brave dangerous waters and use the seashells as ballast; as they unloaded their cargo closer to African markets, like the port town of 'Aydhab, they of course could profit greatly. It is generally hypothesized that these seashells reached West Africa through the well-developed trade routes stretching north of Sahara, rather than being transported across sub-Saharan routes. Evidence supporting this claim come partly in the form of archaeological findings of bags of seashells in the Saharan desert, just north of where the Mali Empire once stood (Garenne-Marot, 2009, p. 4). The main rationale in establishing the direction of that trade lay in the fact that, along with the abandoned seashells were copper rods produced north of the Sahara, headed for sale in the southern areas where copper was demanded. Leo Africanus observed seashell money in the 16th century as far from the coast as Timbuktu (Einzig, 1949, p. 141).

The Indian Hub

What more reason do we have to believe Battúta when he connects seashells in the Maldives with those traded in the far-away interior of Western Africa? It is already established that the Egyptian towns by the Red Sea were important hubs in the Indian trade with Europe and North Africa, and Battúta specifically mentions Bengal as one destination of the seashells exported from the islands. That last claim is partially corroborated by some of the earliest references to seashell money on the Indian subcontinent, which exist in the form of accounts on India and China by two Arab merchants – one living in the 9th century and the other in the 10th century. These references are not clear about the exact geography, but it is considered highly likely that the kingdom they speak of was situated within an area that would lend some support to Battúta's words:

> *Shells are current in this Country [Rahmi], and serve for small Money, notwithstanding that they have Gold and Silver, Wood-Aloes, and Sable-Skins of which they make the Furniture of Saddles and Housings. [...]*

> *All these things [rhino flesh, rhino horns, girdles] are to be purchased in the Kingdom of Rahmi for Shells, which are the current Money. (al-Sīrāfī & Sulaymān, 9th-10th century, pp. 17-18)*

34

In Henry Yule's 1874 version of the recounts of Marco Polo's travels, there are multiple instances of where Polo runs into this phenomenon as well, and where Yule consequently discusses it. We know of these stories due to them being written down by Rustichello da Pisa a few decades before Ibn Battúta set out on his journey. The two Italians were imprisoned together in Genoa during a war between that republic and Venice, and it was during that time Rustichello carefully listened to Polo's accounts of the East, and subsequently published those stories after his imprisonment ended. The first such mention of seashell money is when Polo entered the landlocked province of Carajan, which is modern day Yunnan in China:

> *Their money is such as I will tell you. They use for the purpose certain white porcelain shells that are found in the sea, such as are sometimes put on dogs' collars; and 80 of these porcelain shells pass for a single weight of silver, equivalent to two Venice groats, i.e. 24 piccoli. Also eight such weights of silver count equal to one such weight of gold. (Polo, The Book of Ser Marco Polo, the Venetian Vol II, 1271-1295, p. 39)*

It is not exactly clear what exchange rate this indicated in terms of grams of silver. But Henry Yule does shine some light on later, much worse exchange rates, albeit to the Indian silver rupee and in a slightly different area:

> *The most comprehensive employment of the cowrie currency of which I have ever heard is that described by the Hon. Robert Lindsay as existing in Eastern Bengal during the last century. When that gentleman went as Resident and Collector to Silhet about 1778, cowries constituted nearly the whole currency of the Province. The yearly revenue amounted to 250,000 rupees, and this*

> *was entirely paid in cowries at the rate 5120 to the*
> *rupee. It required large warehouses to contain*
> *them, and when the year's collection was complete*
> *a large fleet of boats to transport them to Dacca.*
> *(Polo, The Book of Ser Marco Polo, the Venetian*
> *Vol II, 1271-1295, p. 44)*

While in the city of Carajan (bearing the same name as the province), Polo described the seashell money again. And here he importantly states the connection to India, which very well could have meant Bengal:

> *In this country gold-dust is found in great*
> *quantities; that is to say in the rivers and lakes,*
> *whilst in the mountains gold is found in pieces of*
> *larger size. Gold is indeed so abundant that they*
> *give one saggio of gold for only six of the same*
> *weight in silver. And for small change they use*
> *the porcelain shells I mentioned before. These are*
> *not found in the country, however, but are*
> *brought from India. (Polo, The Book of Ser Marco*
> *Polo, the Venetian Vol II, 1271-1295, p. 45)*

Moving forward in time a few centuries, it is in Albert Gray's translation of *The Voyage Of Francois Pyrard Vol I*, that the French navigator de Laval corroborates on at least one of the trade routes, as he and his fellow countrymen were shipwrecked and held captive in the Maldives:

> *There is another kind of wealth at the*
> *Maldives, viz, certain little shells containing a*
> *little animal, large as the tip of the little finger,*
> *and quite white, polished, and bright: they are*
> *fished twice a month, three days before and three*
> *days after the new moon, as well as at the full, and*
> *none would be got at any other season. The*

women gather them on the sands and in the
shallows of the sea, standing in the water up to
their waists. They call them Boly, and export to
all parts an infinite quantity, in such wise that in
one year I have seen thirty or forty whole ships
loaded with them without other cargo. All go to
Bengal, for there only is there a demand for a large
quantity at high prices. The people of Bengal use
them for ordinary money, although they have gold
and silver and plenty of other metals; and, what is
more strange, kings and great lords have houses
built expressly to store these shells, and treat them
as part of their treasure. (Pyrard, 1619, pp. 236-
239)

Curiously enough, the only reason the Frenchmen were able to escape their captivity was a Bengal raid on the islands – something which very well might have had to do with the Bengali commanders realizing this is where money was produced and possibly stored. The Maldives were known as *Divah Kavzah*, or "Cowry Islands", after all (Quiggin, 1949, p. 28).

Transportation to the Lands of Scarcity

So in conclusion, it is quite clear that seashells were exported from the Maldives to mainly Bengal, and perhaps other Indian ports as well, only to branch out in northern and eastern routes to Tibet and China (an old Chinese word for seashells, *pei*, later came to mean "money"[13]), and western routes to the coast of East Africa, perhaps through Yemenite ports. It is only logical that the seashells, where they were used as money, in general obtained higher value the further away from their place of origin. Battúta, as we have seen, observed incredible price differences, and there

---

[13] (Quiggin, 1949, p. 225)

are indications that these lasted for many centuries even. Around the time Pyrard and his men had left the Maldives, European traders began exporting seashells not to Bengal or East Africa, but directly to West Africa. Hingston Quiggin referred to A. Churchill's writings:

> *The Boejies, or Cauries [cowries], which the French call Bouges, are small milk-white shells, commonly as big as small olives, and are produced and gather'd among the shoals and rocks of the Maldivy islands, near the coast of Malabar in the East-Indies, and thence transported as ballast to Goa, Cochin, and other ports in the East-Indies, by the natives of those numerous islands: and from the above-nam'd places, are dispersed to the Dutch and English factories in India; then brought over to Europe, more especially by the Dutch, who make a great advantage of them, according to the occasion the several trading nations of Europe have for this trash, to carry on their traffick at the coast of Guinea and of Angola, to purchase slaves or other goods of Africa, and are only proper for that trade, no other people in the universe putting such a value on them as the Guineans, and more especially those of Fida and Ardra have long done, and still do to this very day. (Churchill, 1744, pp. 338-339)*

It may be claimed that the collection of seashells in the Maldives must more often than not have been a very profitable business. But before turning further to the production of this money, it is worth briefly mentioning its emergence and later dethronement in East Africa as well; Paul Einzig has gathered accounts from Germans that detailed exactly this in what is now Uganda – another landlocked area. He writes:

When cowries first made their appearance, they, too, were very valuable. It was possible to buy not only cloth and food but even boats and slaves with cowries. Two cowrie shells would purchase a woman. Subsequently large quantities found their way into the country. They became the principal medium of exchange and were also extensively used as a standard of value. In 1911 the value of a cow was 2 500 cowrie shells, that of a goat was equal to 500 cowries; a fowl was sold for 25 cowrie shells and a cock for 50; an ivory tusk weighing 62 lb sold for 1 000 cowrie shells. [...]

With the penetration of European civilization through the construction of the Uganda Railway, coins gradually took the place of cowries. As a result cowries depreciated. In 1896 cowries were exchanged for about 200 to the rupee, but by 1901 the exchange rate rose to 800. After 31 March 1901, cowries ceased to be acceptable in payment of taxes. At the same time the Government placed an embargo on the import of cowries, having received information that large amounts were being imported from German East Africa. (Einzig, 1949, p. 124)

With seashells now being imported to Africa from the east and west, there was nowhere for the state of relative scarcity of this money to escape anymore, and the money was eventually dethroned in all of these places. Many of these eyewitness accounts fit well in the logical framework discussed earlier in the book, in which seashell money, having just emerged as the most saleable good, is first highly valuable and then falls in value as producers of that money put more hands and capital to the task of providing more units to any market where they make a profit. The ease with which the sea shell money was produced, ultimately put such a severe dent in its price through inflation, that individuals found it uneconomical to continue to use it as a medium of exchange. Since the money lacked *hardness* it was naturally ruined and demonetized in favor of a harder money like silver or gold coins, which the Bengalis at the time of Battúta already happily transacted with. There is one interesting medieval account, mentioned by Alison Hingston Quiggin, which is helpful in further emphasizing this dynamic:

> *Masudi of Baghdad the Arab historian, who died about the middle of the 10th century, amplifies this account [cowrie production]. He records that cowries were the only money in the Maldives, and when the royal treasury was getting empty the Queen directed women to cut branches of coconut palms and throw them on the sea. The animals climbed up on to these and they were collected and spread on the seashore until only empty shells were left, which were brought in to replenish the treasury. (Quiggin, 1949, p. 28)*

Similar resource allocation to further production was always going to be the end-point of seashell money. If becoming money in multiple empires, it follows that the people of the Maldives likely would have set up large-scale production in the form that is most efficient. It is not hard to imagine them constructing whole islands artificially for this purpose in order to profit, either for themselves or for others as slaves.

It is also finally worth emphasizing that before the disruptive waves of monetary inflation, seashells were not bad money, or it would not have emerged as such out of a number of contenders and in multiple societies no less. One hugely underappreciated aspect of this money was the ease of which forgery could be

40

restricted, owing to the uniqueness of the species, and to the natural difficulty in which the shells could be imitated. The initial good monetary properties of seashells is further evidenced by the fact that Native American tribes, isolated from the diligent collectors on the Maldives, and from Indian or Yemenite seafarers, also used such a medium as money, albeit a different species. Instead of inflation through far-away islanders, the Native Americans had it served to them by European settlers that through technological superiority could mass-produce the animal and its shell. In other words, the same lack of hardness of this type of money made itself known there as well.

2. A Trail of Beads

attúta, after realizing he would not be able to reach Mecca through the port town 'Aydhab, had returned to Cairo. From there he continued to the Holy Land and Syria. In what today is southern Turkey, he incidentally took note of a certain *Isma'ilite* sect that possessed many strong fortresses and that he also described as "the arrows of the sultan". He of course refers to the original Assassins, now popularized in books, movies and video games. From Syria, he ventured to Medina and Mecca, and finally fulfilled his first and highly anticipated pilgrimage after having passed the merciless desert of the peninsula's interior:

> *From Tabúk the caravan travels with great speed night and day, for fear of this desert. Halfway through is the valley of al-Ukhaydir, which might be the valley of Hell (may God preserve us from it). One year the pilgrims suffered terribly here from the samoom-wind; the water-supplied dried up and the price of a single drink rose to a thousand dinars, but both seller*

and buyer perished. Their story is written on a
rock in the valley. (Battúta, 1325-1354, p. 73)

While traveling north again across the Arabian Peninsula, he and fellow pilgrims heard of a very recent attack on a group of dervishes (Sufi believers) by Arab brigands. But having escaped such dangers, Battúta and his company soon enough reached Baghdad, a town that impressed him despite having suffered desolation during recent Mongol invasions. The company also passed Basra, headed deep into Persia – then governed by the Mongols as well – and then took a detour northwest into Kurdish lands. Ibn Battúta had by now sworn to not, if possible, travel any road twice. Excluding Mecca in this, he proceeded towards that city soon enough for a second pilgrimage.

Opaque Beginnings

The story of glass bead money first loosely intertwines with Ibn Battúta's journey after he set out south from Mecca, towards the East African coast. Leaving Arab towns behind him, he ventured around the horn of Africa, hugged the mainland until he reached The Coast Lands, or *as-Sawáhil* as they were called by the Arabs. It was in the Swahili cities that glass beads – a rather mystical type of money – were later imported. It should be noted that, as with the seashell money already discussed, Battúta might at that point have had no clue that such bead money even existed. The first time he mentions beads is much later on his journeys, while traveling the western parts of sub-Saharan Africa:

> *A traveller in this country carries no*
> *provisions, whether plain food or seasonings, and*
> *neither gold nor silver. He takes nothing but*
> *pieces of salt and glass ornaments, which the*
> *people call beads, and some aromatic goods.*
> *(Battúta, 1325-1354, p. 322)*

43

Battúta's company, while travelling south from Timbuktu in that late stage of his many travels, purchased goods with such glass beads each night. The story of how glass beads ended up in 14th century West Africa in the first place is a rather opaque one. It has been speculated that the Phoenicians of Carthage, while setting up colonies and trading stations along the West-African coast, introduced beads made of colorful Mediterranean coral to the locals, in exchange for goods of higher standing among Phoenicians. There are extensive but later evidence[14] of coral fisheries in the Mediterranean, for example on Sardinia, Sicily, Corsica, Majorca and in Catalonia. A number of these areas were colonized and subsequently controlled by Carthage over long periods of time. Furthermore, the Amber route, stretching from the Baltic Sea to the Black Sea, supplied the Mediterranean societies with beautiful amber beads that likely found their way further south as well.

As the technology of glass making advanced in medieval Egypt and thereafter spread to parts of Europe – particularly Venice – it has also been speculated that glass beads became a rather convenient bastardization of valuable coral beads, and perhaps amber beads or gem stones in general. The inhabitants of parts of Western Africa, having dealt with scarce, colorful coral beads for perhaps hundreds of years, and with various scarce, uncut gemstones obtained from native riverbeds or open mines, did likely not have the proper knowledge to assess the state of abundance of this latest wave of beautiful glass. A heuristic that once worked well for them, had with better technology in the countries of the Mediterranean been transformed into a severe weakness. A similar vulnerability likely existed among the peoples of the Himalayas, as objects from the far-away sea were naturally scarce there:

---

[14] (Tavernier, 1678, p. 151)

> *The coral which is carried from our parts of the*
> *world [the Mediterranean] has a better sale here*
> *[in Himalaya] than in any other country. (Polo,*
> *The Book of Ser Marco Polo, the Venetian Vol I,*
> *1271-1295, p. 159)*

Hingston Quiggin found that coral beads were used as money in parts of Tibet as late as the 20th century (Quiggin, 1949, p. 223).

Trade-routes to the Interior

With the discussed evolution of coral- and glass beads in mind, it is now worth exploring the work of Karin Pallaver, who on behalf of the British Museum researched the extensive 19th century use of glass beads on caravan routes stretching from the east coast of modern day Tanzania, to the large lakes in the country's western interior. In observations of those networks lie likely clues to why exactly Battúta observed this type of money and why it is no longer anywhere to be found as such. It may also help explain why Battúta observed both seashell money and glass bead money in such close proximity of one another.

Pallaver starts her work by describing a couple of shifting dynamics in the 19th century East African trade networks. The monsoon winds of the Indian Ocean had for centuries taken goods from India and the Arabian Peninsula to Zanzibar and likely to the very towns cluttering the coast of East Africa that Battúta had visited. Meanwhile, trade between Africa's interior and these coastal towns had been limited at best. As demand for slave labor rose in the 18th and 19th century, and as Europe and India slowly started to appreciate East African ivory in full, this led market mechanics to push for more and larger trade connections between the coast and the interior. The Nyamwezi people was one of the groups quick to seize on this new opportunity (Pallaver, 2009, p. 20).

As for the monetary systems used along those trade routes, they were complex. Maria Theresa silver thalers, named after the 18th century Empress of Austria, Hungary and Bohemia, were used in the coastal towns and on Zanzibar. As were the coexisting Indian silver rupee and the Spanish piastre silver dollar. While these more conventional types of money were demanded in the east, trade caravans had to stock up on commodities before leaving for the interior. The most common of these commodities were, according to Pallaver's sources, cloth, glass beads and metal wires – all of which European observers sometimes referred to as "African money". The metal wire money especially proved an inconvenience to the European Post- and Telegraph Offices in Tanganyika as locals had a habit of stealing that good due to its inflated value (Einzig, 1949, p. 131). Yet it was especially cloths that were used by the caravans to bribe their way through the territories of certain chiefs (something which would have been familiar to Ibn Battúta, as we shall see later in his journeys).

Second only to the cloth goods in demand were glass beads; this demand was especially high far inland close to Lake Victoria and Lake Tanganyika. The supply of glass beads to the caravans was initially monopolized by Zanzibar-based Indian traders, who according to sources imported these beads to the island by the tonnes. These beads trickled out to the various trade networks, towards places where they ultimately were scarcer and more valuable. To quote Pallaver:

> [...] among the most requested there were the
> same same, or sami-sami beads, made of red coral,
> the white beads, popularly known as merikani, the
> gulabi beads made of pink porcelain, the black
> beads called bubu, the sungomaji, white and blue
> beads produced in Nurmberg, and a variety called
> sofi, Venetian cylindrical beads available in
> different colours. (Pallaver, 2009)

Pallaver bundling in coral beads with the rest is an interesting footnote, as it lends support to the theory that the bead trade might have emerged first through the trade of goods like genuine coral, only to be followed by replicas. Yet another vague connection to mythical scarcity was the belief among some tribes that certain beads grew and bred in the very earth itself – likely a result of individuals having found hidden and forgotten bead treasures buried in the ground of abandoned village sites (Quiggin, 1949, p. 38).

The Bead Puzzle

Sir Henry Morton Stanley, in his 1871 work *How I Found Livingstone*, elaborated on these bead-based monetary systems that he had had the privilege to run into while traveling the interior. He found that the red *sami-sami* would be readily taken in Unyamwezi, the black *bubu* in Ugogo, the egg *sungomazzi* in Ujiji and Uguhham, and the white *Merikani* in Ufipa, Usagara and Ugogo. If valuable in one regional area, the beads were often worthless in many others. (Stanley, 1890, p. 28)

Not only did different tribes accept different types of beads; this puzzle changed dramatically with time as well, which made the matter even more complicated. Merchants caught owning certain types of beads for too long could see their entire wealth evaporate as those beads fell out of fashion for one reason or another. English explorers Speke and Burton apparently managed to hold one type of beads long enough that they were unable to even give them away as gifts (Pallaver, 2009, p. 25). Henry Morton Stanley complained about this as well:

> *The various kind of beads required great time to learn, for the women of Africa are as fastidious in their tastes for beads as the women of New York are for jewelry. The measures also had to be mastered, which, seeing that it was an entirely*

new business in which I was engaged, were rather
complicated, and perplexed me considerably for a
time. (Bennett, 1970, p. 5)

Paul Einzig's sources mention similar difficulties. One expedition found its black porcelain beads were met with contempt, and after having traded some of its porcelain beads to small blue ones at a considerable loss, the expedition found that the natives suddenly demanded the former (Einzig, 1949, p. 130). Other travelers found that while rose-colored beads were popular, sea-green and white ones were refused, and red ones were rejected as to only fit uncivilized peoples in the north (Quiggin, 1949, p. 101). In any case, as soon as the trade caravans had reached the lakes, they generally had sold most of their imported goods, with especially the beads fetching many times the market price on Zanzibar. Personnel costs and tributes on the way back to the coast were mostly paid for in goods acquired in the interior.

Pallaver makes an interesting observation of the fact that the trade route economy rested mainly on three different monies. Cloths, being the most sought after goods in the interior, were used mainly for high-value transactions like slaves or ivory, while beads and copper wires were, often but not exclusively, used for smaller ones. This, of course, is not random, but the result of saleableness considerations with regards to transactions of differing sizes, just as coins of differing precious metal contents facilitated similar efficiency improvements in more developed parts of the world.

Now, as it is clear what the trade caravans brought in to the interior, and what they subsequently brought back to the coast, let's look a bit closer on especially the glass beads. A common misconception is that Europeans were the deceitful, imperialistic initiators of supplying glass beads to this specific area. The first beads in East Africa, according to Pallaver, originated from East Asia, and the initial attempts to introduce for example Venetian beads apparently failed as no one accepted them as money. Even as Henry Morton Stanley managed to match the supplied bead types with what the locals actually demanded, he noticed to his probable disappointment that some of his beads could buy him vegetables, but not eggs, milk or fowl.

Luckily, in some of the larger financial centers in proximity to the caravan routes (for example Tabora and Ujiji) existed markets where all beads fetched prices in relation to one another. Beads could also in these cities be used to buy food, among other things. German explorer Hermann von Wissmann observed that in the Ujiji market the smallest coins were represented by red and blue glass beads. Cotton cloths and copper represented silver money, whereas slaves, cattle and ivory represented gold. The explorer Joseph Thomson corroborated this as he documented his visit to the market of Ujiji (Thomson, 1881, p. 90).

Pallaver also mentions the missionary Edward C. Hore, who had this to say about the Ujiji beads:

> *Here for the first time we find a regular currency or money in use by the natives; it consists of strings of blue and white cylindrical beads, each string containing 20 beads. Bunches of 10 strings are called "fundo". From 9 to 11 fundo are given in exchange for 4 yards of good heavy American calico; the value varying daily, according to the quantity of cloth in the market. (Hore, 1883, p. 9)*

As information on the intricate glass bead trade networks trickled back to Europe and beyond, it became clear that the way to upend them with an inflow of new supply in order to profit was not as straightforward a path as one might have thought. As already mentioned, certain Venetian beads had initially been rejected, so it was established that the African tribes were not going to accept just any type of round glass objects coming their way when their century old bead networks at the time consisted of dozens, if not hundreds of different bead types[15]. This was of course a cause of annoyance among Europeans, some of whom attributed it to the vanity of African women, as is anecdotally indicated by Sir Stanley's comment on their changing taste for beads. It is likely that the ever changing demand of bead types instead was a result of economic realities, like monetary inflation – in other words logical from an economical point of view. The glass replicas of corals, pearls and stones had slowly but surely eroded trust in the scarcity of many of these monies. Pallaver has found a source in the German explorer J. M. Hildebrandt, which aptly may represent this sobering realization:

> *Bartering with goods is a terrible business. In Europe it is generally thought that the savages of Inner Africa accept a string of beads or a yard of cloth as a sufficient recompense for dozens of elephants' teeth, and that the nourishment of a caravan is repaid by the honour of the visit. These happy days are long since passed. The savages have advanced from the state of childhood to the years of hobble-de-hoyhood. (Rigby, 1878, p. 452)*

Venetian Mechanization

The happy days may indeed have been over for Hildebrandt, but not for the Europeans more broadly. Building from the expertise stretching back to medieval times, Venetian bead production was by this time an ever increasing juggernaut that from the middle of the 19th century started serious mechanization efforts. These efforts greatly affected output, and was combined with Venetian officials forbidding, on pain of death, the city's bead producers to spread any knowledge about production processes. Apart

---

[15] Einzig puts the number as high as 400. (Einzig, 1949, p. 130)

from the earlier mentioned initial failed efforts to penetrate the complicated East African bead market, the Venetians, according to Pallaver, evidently succeeded based on documented export numbers from the Venetian Chamber of Commerce. Their production centers still had to regularly change the glass bead types every year (sometimes almost monthly), which of course was a real but not insurmountable problem for them. Curiously, the glass bead export was higher to neighboring European countries as well as to India, where they were not used as money, but as accessories on clothes for example. This export is also partially explained by the fact that the beads often continued their journey to Africa from the foreign ports instead.

At the end of the bead trail is the conclusion that helps explain why Battúta and his fellow travelers could buy essential provisions with beads, while nowadays it is impossible. This conclusion helps explain why, from being worth their weight in gold in the 19th century Gold Coast (Einzig, 1949, p. 154), *aggri* beads are today essentially worthless. The one fatal flaw – an ultimate end-point of most monies – was of course that they would eventually be mass produced, causing high inflation on tribes saving and earning their livelihood in that exact money. As technology advanced and the cost to produce beautiful glass beads from abundant, cheap sand continuously decreased, the room for ever higher profits by producers increased as long as people continued to use these beads as money. The effects of monetization, discussed in the book's first chapter, has to be remembered: money is always valued at a premium due to its use also as an exceptionally good medium of exchange. With the production cost cuts, a larger part of this premium could be pocketed.

It should finally be added that glass beads, like seashells discussed earlier, often had many good monetary properties temporarily superior to those of other commodities traded in the regions of the interior (like bulky iron horse shoes or deteriorating bags of millet). Coming in strings, they were in effect divisible. They were also relatively fungible, easy to carry and exchange, did not easily break or deteriorate, and they were easy to use as a unit of account. The lack of hardness, however, had them dethroned as money in province after province. Despite the documented instances where East Africans constantly tried to adopt new types of beads as money, the Venetian seigniorage ultimately caught up with them, and in the fullness of time they had to abandon this type of money altogether in order not to face further poverty or – in the worst case – slavery due to the inability of defending themselves from tribes or nations with harder monies.

3. Money of the Steppes

Returning from East African cities like Kilwa and Mombasa, Ibn Battúta now aspired to make the pilgrimage to Mecca once more. But despite having already been in danger multiple times on his journeys, he now entered an extensive period of misfortunes. In an attempt to reach the Strait of Hormuz, his company was caught in a violent storm, sinking the ship in front of him. Battúta disembarked upon reaching a village, possibly to escape the horrors on the sea, but again found himself in danger due to a dishonest guide. For the whole hot journey to the town of Qalhát in modern day Oman, the explorer spent the night fully awake, with sword in hand, in fear of being murdered. But he did survive both thirst and treachery, and by later crossing the desert in a westward direction he again reached Mecca.

Ibn Battúta's third journey may be considered his most interesting one, as it would take him to the Far East – a place which few in the West could even dream of visiting. It started, however, by again passing through the Holy Land. He continued through Anatolia where Turks recently had been busy occupying

Greek cities and towns, and later also found time to visit the metropolis Constantinople.

Remnants of a Nomad Past

Battúta also visited multiple towns in the less civilized parts around the Black Sea. He went to the Genoese city of Kaffa, in what today is Crimea, by enduring severe storms that almost capsized the ship. Curiously, it appears Battúta and his company were unused to the loud ringing of church bells, because as the predominantly Christian city suddenly rang with them, they took to the rooftop of their housing in confusion and loudly called for prayer. Muslims living in Kaffa quickly calmed Battúta and stopped him from accidentally conjuring up a religious brawl. From Kaffa he set out on the vast grass plains towards the Caspian and Aral Sea. As he traveled to meet with Sultan Muhammad Úzbeg Khán (Öz Beg Khan) of the Golden Horde – a powerful Turco-Mongol ruler that Battúta claims had been busy warring with the Byzantine Empire – the nomadic background of these Mongols soon made itself apparent:

> We set out [from Kaffa] with the amir
> Tuluktumúr and his brother and two sons. At
> every halt the Turks loose there horses, oxen and
> camels, and drive them out to pastures at liberty,
> night or day, without shepherds or guardians.
> This is due to the severity of their laws against
> theft. Any person found in possession of a stolen
> horse is obliged to restore it with nine others; if he
> cannot do this, his sons are taken instead, and if
> he has no sons he is slaughtered like a sheep.
> (Battúta, 1325-1354, p. 143)

Livestock had for a long time been the money of various Mongol and Tartar tribes, and although the Golden Horde at the time of Battúta's visit operated mostly under silver dirhams, his note on

54

livestock fines likely revealed one remnant of such systems. Similar traces could be observed as soon as he reached Sarai, the capital of the Golden Horde:

> *The day after my arrival I visited him [the Sultan] in the afternoon at a ceremonial audience; a great banquet was prepared and we broke our fast in his presence. These Turks do not follow the custom of assigning a lodging to visitors and giving them money for their expenses, but they send him sheep and horses for slaughtering and skins of qumizz [curdled milk], which is their form of benefaction. (Battúta, 1325-1354, p. 148)*

It should be mentioned that Battúta, on his long travels, received money from local rulers almost everywhere he went, even in some non-Muslim kingdoms. These Mongols, while utilizing coined silver, likely still carried strong influences of past livestock monetary systems when giving gifts as well.

Paul Einzig has much to say about the historic livestock standard of the Mongols. He emphasizes that the, by far, most important money used by them, was their animals. Even as prisoners were taken and ransomed for silver or gold, and even as they looted hoards of such metals, trade among the Mongols themselves were often conducted in livestock (Einzig, 1949, p. 283). British soldier and author of *The Quest for Cathay*, Percy Sykes, corroborated on similar monetary systems as late as the 19th century, as he was stationed by the Pamir Mountains. Here is what he had to say about the use of sheep money among the people he met there:

> *Among the Kirghiz whom I met on the Pamirs the difficulty always was for the young fellows to find the hundred sheep which was the usual price for a girl, and one of my hunters, when paid off,*

counted his wages as representing so many sheep!
(Sykes, 1936, p. 103)

Einzig has a number of references to sheep money as well. He found that in Tibet, they were used to measure value – in other words a unit of account. In Mongolia and other parts of Central Asia, sheep served as a unit of account as well, and the monetary system even dealt with different denominations. A grown-up bull was worth ten grown-up rams, twenty grown-up sheep, thirty one-year-old sheep, or sixty lambs. (Einzig, 1949, p. 108)

Yet another telling example of remnants of a livestock standard in modern Mongolia, is reference by Hingston-Quiggin:

> *A traveller once asked a patriarch owner of several thousand horses why he did not sell some every year. He replied, 'Why sell what I delight in? I do not need money. If I had any I would shut it up in a box where no one would see it. But when my horses run over the plain everyone sees them and knows that they are mine and is reminded that I am rich'. (Quiggin, 1949, p. 277)*

Civilizations in Transformation

Livestock standards of the past often provides valuable examples of monetary systems in transformation. Not only did some of the early coins depict the very animals that they likely replaced – metal coinage and livestock often operated as money in parallel. Einzig, upon researching the money of the Hittites, noted:

> *To judge by a code of law originating from the 14th century B.C., weighed silver played the part of currency during that period in the Hittite Empire. A very advanced system of price fixing appears to have been in force. The unit was the*

> shekel, or rather the half-shekel, in terms of which
> prices and wages were fixed in the code. The price
> of meat provided the only noteworthy exception
> from this rule. It was fixed in terms of sheep and
> fractions of sheep instead of silver. This seems to
> indicate the existence of a sheep-unit during an
> earlier period. (Einzig, 1949, p. 219)

Studying the history of the Persians (whose ancestors were nomads) provides similar examples. Einzig:

> Oxen and sheep were the original standard of
> value in Ancient Persia and were also used as
> medium of exchange. There is evidence in the
> Zend Avesta that they were confined to be used as
> currency concurrently with metals. A doctor's
> fees were fixed in terms of animals or parts of
> animals according to the standard of the patient.
> (Einzig, 1949, p. 227)

Another circumstance of an older sheep-standard is provided by the Jews who historically transacted in *kesitah*. Although it is no longer known what exactly a *kesitah* represented, etymology (and early Greek translations of the Bible) suggest it was a coin bearing the impression of a lamb, or just a measure of the amount of silver equal to the price of a lamb. That the word *mikhne* means, or at least meant, both "livestock" and "purchase" lends further support to the theory (Einzig, 1949, p. 220).

Ancient Greece likely operated on parallel monies as well. Various copper ingots in the shape of ox hides were thought to have first represented such a commodity as some even had one side mimicking the hairy part of the hide, and the other side mimicking the raw inside (Quiggin, 1949, p. 272). The Iliad and the Odyssey both provide references to the use of oxen as a unit of account. Einzig also mentions a curious phrase used in the 6th and 5th century B.C. to describe someone having been bribed to keep silent: "[having] an ox on his tongue" (Einzig, 1949, p. 229). Finally, it is thought that the marks of oxen and sheep on early Roman bronze- and copper coinage represented similar links between an older system on livestock money, and that of metallic coinage (Einzig, 1949, p. 236).

War Externalities

Furthermore, it is important to understand that money, in some regards, is not uniform in its externalities. An appreciation in the value of livestock money, for example, has other externalities than an appreciation in the value of gold. History has shown us that gold vaults and mines have been obvious military objectives in war, and a price increase of that money magnifies the temptation to capture storage- and production centers. As Nick Szabo bluntly put it: "Aztecs took gold tribute from their subject tribes. Spanish conquistadors looted the Aztecs. Sir Francis Drake looted Spanish galleons. Seizing gold vaults was a universal war objective."

The gold of nation states have always been defended by strategically located armies or militias. But what do people do when the very land they walk on belongs to the sphere of the production of money of their warlike neighbors? It is likely that this phenomenon manifested itself among the many Mongol tribes in Eurasia, who for a long period of time appear to have operated on livestock money. If livestock was money, it must have had a premium on its value due to the added utility of facilitating economic exchange. Any such premium would, given all else equal, put an upward pressure on the amount of capital allocated toward production or collection as it made it more profitable to breed or in other ways obtain livestock. In other words, if their own graze-lands were not enough, this premium gave direct economic incentives for the Mongols to aggressively conquer new graze-lands.

Much evidence of Mongol livestock-money admittedly stems from the 19th and 20th century, but it is highly likely that the Mongols utilized a similar standard before conquering China and other more civilized nations. The slaughter they brought with them as they trampled these other societies was on a scale seldom seen before; it is estimated that many millions died as a result of systematic executions and deliberate starvation. Einzig makes this very point:

> There can be no doubt that this search for new grazing lands was largely responsible for the aggressive expansionary policy of the pastoral races which were surging westward towards the end of the Ancient Period, and in particular of the Mongols towards the middle of the 13th century. It was largely because they chose to use livestock as their currency that they had to find more and more room for their livestock which tended to be well in excess of normal economic requirements. (Einzig, 1949, pp. 283-284)

A similar aggression-dynamic was to be found in the overstocking of cattle money among the Colombian Indians (Einzig, 1949, p. 187).

Some would argue that the ruthlessness of the Mongols was game-theoretic; any new foe knew what happened if they did not surrender. But this cannot be the only explanation of the mass murdering, or other nations and tribes would have historically been equally harsh after subjugating their neighbors. Henry Yule has a brief excerpt on the Mongol conquest of Balkh in northeastern Persia, which lends support against the game-theory argument:

> Balk, "the mother of cities," suffered mercilessly from Chinghiz. Though the city had yielded without resistance, the whole population

> *was marched by companies into the plain, on the*
> *usual Mongol pretext of counting them, and then*
> *brutally massacred. (Polo, The Book of Ser Marco*
> *Polo, the Venetian Vol I, 1271-1295, p. 143)*

This livestock-money externality described here seems in other words plausible enough to warrant mentioning. The dethroning of livestock money, however, may have been caused not by this externality, nor by a lack of hardness, but due to rising storage costs as the nomads settled down in cities such as Sarai. A similar storage cost argument was brought forward also by Carl Menger[16]. So, the very money that once pushed men to war, can be said to have been tamed, just as the nomads were when they slowly chose to settle.

---

[16] (Menger, Principles of Economics, 1871, p. 265)

4. Fur in the 'Land of Darkness'

After traveling some of the dominions of the Golden Horde, it must have been clear to Ibn Battúta how high a standing animals had in Mongol culture. He would then not have been surprised to discover traces of a similar reverence further north, among the Russian peoples and their neighbors. Paul Einzig details the evolution of animal-related money in medieval Russia, where inhabitants from a very early period had intertwined the concept of money with their animals.

Silent Trade beyond the Ice Desert

While Battúta did not visit any Russian cities, he does mention a curious economic phenomenon in the north known as *silent trade,* which the Russians likely had to deal with as well:

> *I had heard of the city of Bulghár and desired to visit it, in order to see for myself what they tell of the extreme shortness of the night there and also the shortness of the day in the opposite season. It*

61

was ten nights' journey from the sultan's camp,
so I requested that he would give me a guide to
take me to it, and he did so. We reached it in the
month of Ramadán, and when we had breakfasted
after the sunset prayer we had just sufficient time
for night prayers before dawn. I stayed for three
days. I had intended to visit the Land of Darkness
[northern Siberia], which is reached from Bulghár
after a journey of forty days, but I renounced the
project in view of the difficulty of the journey and
the small profit to be got out of it. The only way of
reaching it is to travel on sledges drawn by dogs,
for the desert being covered with ice, neither man
nor beast can walk on it without slipping, whereas
the dogs have claws that grip the ice. [...]

When the travellers have completed forty
stages they alight at the Darkness. Each one of
them leaves the goods he has brought there and
they return to their usual camping-ground. Next
day they go back to seek their goods, and find
opposite them skins of sable, minever, and ermine.
If the merchant is satisfied with the exchange he
takes them, but if not he leaves them. The
inhabitants then add more skins, but sometimes
they take away their goods and leave the
merchant's. This is their method of commerce.
Those who go there do not know whom they are
trading with or whether they be jinn or men, for
they never see anyone. (Battúta, 1325-1354, pp.
150-151)

Einzig emphasizes the use of domesticated reindeer as money in
northern Siberia, but mentions skins and small furs as well
(Einzig, 1949, p. 116). Exactly to what extent the tribes there at

that time used furs and skins as money is unclear. Battúta did, however, receive such goods from the Mongols before heading back towards Constantinople:

> He [the sultan] gave her [the Greek princess] permission and then I too asked him to allow me to go in her company to see Constantinople the Great. He demurred, fearing for my safety, but I said, "I shall go under your patronage and protection and I shall have nothing to fear from anyone." Thereupon he gave me permission and we bade him farewell. He presented me with 1 500 dinars, a robe, and a large number of horses, and each khátún [princess] gave me ingots of silver. The sultan's daughter gave me more than they did, along with a robe and a horse, so I found myself in possession of a considerable quantity of horses, garments, and furs of sable and minever. (Battúta, 1325-1354, pp. 151-152)

While passing close to the border of the Russians, Battúta mentions them mining silver (though this is still doubtful according to some researchers) and casting it into ingots, which functioned as money in the area. As ingots also were part of the gift from the princesses, it is clear that the whole region was in a drawn out transition phase from more primitive monies, to modern coinage.

Etymological Evidence

Some of the evidence of Russian fur money lie in the Russian language; the oldest known Russian word for both "treasure" and "cattle", according to Einzig, is skot, which very likely is related to the old Germanic word for "treasure" and "cattle", skatta (its local variations are still commonly used in Scandinavia today). The same relationship can be observed in the old Russian word for "cattle yard" or "stable", as well as for "treasury": *skotniza*. Where did this linguistic, cross-cultural merge of cattle and money come from? Although likely in place before Viking traders and warriors penetrated deep into Russia where they established trade networks and states, the earliest etymological evidence of Russian cattle money, according to Einzig, stems from this period. The Scandinavians and Russians, in other words, all valued their animals dearly.

Yet, livestock money was suboptimal when trade converged to cities, which may have been what ultimately caused skins and furs to be used as money. The properties of furs and skins that made that commodity suitable enough were: it was of course relatively scarce and hard to acquire, more divisible and naturally standardized, easier to transport, easy to verify the genuineness of, and did not deteriorate quickly. And perhaps most important, it was much easier and cheaper to store than livestock. The existence of such fur money in Russia is independently corroborated by various medieval travelers and authors, but as with the case of livestock money, further evidence is also found in etymology, according to Einzig:

> *In addition to contemporary written evidence there is also etymological evidence in support of the claim that furs and skins were the currency of medieval Russia. The word kuna, which was used to express money in general, originated from the skin of the marten (kunitza). In fact, marten skins were the monetary unit in Russia till the late Middle Ages. It was not until 1409 that the kuna standard was abolished in Pskow, and it existed till 1411 in Novgorod. (Einzig, 1949, pp. 278-279)*

The word *kuna*, although as mentioned stemming from the wild martens, was applied to silver money as well. Having little silver production themselves, the Russians initially imported Arab silver *dirhams* from the south and referred to them not as *dirhams* but as *kuna*. Later, with the influx of Western European silver coins, the *denarius* became known as *kuna*. There appears, according to Einzig, to have existed a somewhat lasting fixed exchange rate between the silver coins and the actual marten skins (5 *kuna* coins to 2 *kunitza* skins), as silver coins were often deemed to be lacking in enough supply to facilitate trade efficiently.

Russian Fractional Reserve Banking

For a long time, the furs had to be complete; claws, paws or snots missing would often result in the fur not being accepted as payment. These standards were relaxed as the central or local governments managing fur storage facilities introduced what appears to be some sort of fractional reserve banking; a much smaller, circular-shaped, Government stamped piece of fur money started to circulate and could allegedly be redeemed for a complete fur at a later time. Hingston-Quiggin mentions the heaviness of bundles of skins and consequent Russian tokenization by using snouts or ears (Quiggin, 1949, p. 188). Einzig complains about the lack of solid evidence of the actual redemption process, but it seems likely such should have been in place or merchants would not have deposited their furs. He also purely attributes this systemic shift to the supply of complete skins not managing to keep up with the pace of expanding monetary requirements. Be that as it may, it is quite possible that the practice instead was introduced in order to have the storage facilities lend out more fur money than they actually had backing for – in other words, the fur storage administrators, like their later gold storage counterparts, had financial incentives to move away from full reserves.

It is possible that Russian bankers and traders profited for a time under this monetary regiment, but Einzig is also quick to add one of the alleged conclusions of that experiment –a loss of faith in this new fur money spread over Russia, especially in the east where extensive trade was conducted with Mongol tribes. The Mongols, wanting little to do with this new kind of stamped fur-pieces, refused commerce:

> *A crisis is said to have occurred, however, when the Mongol invaders of Russia refused to recognize the small bits of fur serving as money. There was general bankruptcy among the merchants. Therefore north-eastern Russia reverted to the use of whole skins with full intrinsic value, in the place of pieces. (Einzig, 1949, p. 280)*

The Russian states, especially after Muscovite centralization efforts, later moved to a mainly gold- and silver based monetary system, but the remains of their fur money concept lived on in memory, and in the names of smaller coin denominations:

> *Hare skins are also believed to have served as a currency. This is deduced from the name of the smallest of early Russian coins, the polushka (quarter copeck). Ushka means 'hare skin', pol signifies 'half', therefore polushka must have been equated to two coins per hare's skin; the latter is said to have been one of the lowest units of exchange before the use of metallic money. (Einzig, 1949, p. 279)*

Polushkas were minted on and off until 1916, just before the Romanov dynasty ended.

Before we move on to other monies, it is important to realize how the Russian money production would have looked like as time passed, in a case of a prolonged fur standard with or without fractional reserve banking. Instead of having thousands of miners looking for precious metals in Russian mountains, there would have been thousands of hunters gathering as many highly valued skins as they could get their hands on. And with the fantastically large forests of Russia, it is likely the monetary inflation would have been considerable over an extended period of time, causing the money to be vulnerable to the very dethronement dynamics that later had heavy, burdensome copper phased out as well.

5. Coconuts of Nicobar

After leaving the dominions of the Golden Horde and then the Chagatai Khanate, Battúta and his fellow travelers reached the Sultanate of Delhi – a powerful empire with its base in northern India. There he was employed by the Sultan (of which we shall speak more of later on), and ultimately sent to China as ambassador. While awaiting embarkation from Calicut, Battúta's hopes of reaching China quickly disappeared as a storm sank many of the ships, including the one on which the present from the Sultan of Delhi was stored. As he had no further way of catching agreeable winds that season, he had to accept that the visit to China had to be put on hold. Having lost some of his own wealth at sea, Battúta first visited the Maldives (he did not dare return to Delhi on account of the first trip's failure) and was treated generously due to his now close relation to the powerful Sultanate in the north. And so, it was only on his second try in reaching China that he passed the Nicobars – a group of tropical islands east of India. As the ship never anchored there, it is highly unlikely that Battúta ever heard of the islands' money, but if he did, he might have been as fascinated as when he saw coconuts for the first time, in Arabian Dhofar:

> *The coco-palm is one of the strangest of trees,*
> *and looks exactly like a date-palm. The nut*
> *resembles a man's head, for it has marks like eyes*
> *and a mouth, and the contents, when it is green,*
> *are like the brains. It has fibre like hair, out of*
> *which they make ropes, which they use instead of*
> *nails to bind their ships together and also as*
> *cables. (Battúta, 1325-1354, p. 114)*

Foreign Traders

The coconuts did of course not function as money in Dhofar but very likely did at this time on the Nicobar Islands. Car Nicobar is a rather solitary speck of land situated in this group, and Paul Einzig has researched its money. One of his sources is George Whitehead, British Government Agent on the island at the start of the 20th century. Whitehead wrote a full book about Car Nicobar, its people, and their customs.

Coconuts were for a long period of time the main staple food and drink on Car Nicobar. The lack of fresh water on the island caused the inhabitants to routinely drink from coconuts and then eat their contents. These coconuts were also the island's main export, and so important to the Nicobarese that they had seven words for it – one for each stage of the nut's development. In the foreword to Whitehead's *In The Nicobar Islands*, Chief Commissioner of the Andaman and Nicobar Islands, R.C. Temple, noted:

> *They [the Nicobarese] will not cultivate*
> *cereals, because the coco-nut supplies practically*
> *all their needs, either directly or as an article of*
> *barter. Also, because it acts as a sufficient*
> *currency, they have no use for money as*

> *Europeans understand it. The coco-nuts are their*
> *money, and though they will not cultivate in the*
> *European sense, they are quick at making gardens*
> *of fruit that grows easily. (Whitehead, 1914, p. 9)*

English zoologist C. Boden Kloss corroborated this claim as he set foot on Car Nicobar around the same time, at the start of the 20th century:

> *These [the children] are very helpful in*
> *climbing the coco palms for the nuts required for*
> *barter, and they are of much assistance to the*
> *foreign traders also, who, to induce the boys to aid*
> *them, supply them with food, and give them*
> *presents of tobacco and other things. (Kloss, 1903,*
> *p. 59)*

Under British colonial rule, many Indian, Burmese and Chinese traders set up shop on the island. Their stores, according to Einzig, offered the islanders tobacco, rice, cloths, lamp oil, cutlery, pots and pans and other useful items, while taking only coconuts in exchange. Commodity prices were often quoted in coconuts as well, making it a unit of account in most barter situations. And sometimes wages were denominated in coconuts. Slightly worse was this money's storage capabilities. The foreign traders built safes consisting of open outdoor areas sealed off by palm leave fences, to store large numbers of coconuts in preparation for incoming trading vessels. Revealing a negative property of edible money, these enclosures were at times looted by hungry pigs who had strong enough jaws to open the coconuts. Boden Kloss had the following to report on the traders, their origin and on the trade in general:

> *The merchants arrive in various kinds of*
> *vessels, from large barquentines, brigs,*
> *brigantines, and schooners, to the baglas of the*

> *Indians and Burmese kallus of 20 or 30 tons.*
> *These come mostly from Calcutta, Bombay,*
> *Negapatam, and Moulmein. The Chinese, of*
> *course, come in their national junks, via*
> *Singapore, Acheen, or Penang. Trade is carried on*
> *by barter; coconuts are the standard of value, and*
> *although dollars and rupees change hands, they*
> *are employed by the natives more as ornaments*
> *than mediums of exchange. The annual*
> *production of coconuts is believed to reach at the*
> *lowest estimate, 15 000 000; about one-third of*
> *which are exported and the remainder consumed*
> *and planted. (Kloss, 1903, p. 253)*

The use of coconuts as money was deemed slightly problematic by the British, who halfheartedly tried to infuse the island economy with Indian silver rupees instead. This was logical as coconuts naturally deteriorated and thus silver could help the Nicobarese to dispose of their nuts at the moment they became ripe, instead of holding on to them for monetary reasons. The monetization attempts were generally unsuccessful – perhaps due to cultural reasons – though rupees were, as indicated in Kloss's writing, sometimes used as jewelry. The slow silver money adoption might have been a natural result of abundant defrauding by traders in the form of fake silver cutlery, as the islanders had no way of properly assessing the various metals (Einzig, 1949, p. 111). Such frauds are mentioned by Hingston Quiggin as well (Quiggin, 1949, p. 200).

Debts and Inflation

Perhaps also due to cultural reasons, many Nicobarese accumulated mountains of debt to the foreign traders, and at some point millions of coconuts were owed on certain islands. Whitehead attributes this phenomenon to a general honesty among the population, and to their reluctance to decline offers of postponed payments to the traders. A certain "Mr Crow" (likely a name given to this specific native by British sailors in the past) complained about this to Whitehead:

> *They make us have the things. I don't want them; and I have no nuts now. Can't I send the things back again to the shop? (Whitehead, 1914, p. 81)*

Since the Indian Civil Code did not fully run on the islands, the traders had no legal way to obtain Nicobarese land or property in the event of a debtor failing to pay back his coconut-denominated loan. They instead had to rely on the general willingness to pay back. In any case, after seeing debt spiral out of control multiple times, the British authorities declared coconut-lending illegal and all purchases had to be made cash down – in coconuts that is. This policy, however, was not strictly enforced.

Coconuts continued to be used as money, and interestingly, they seem at first glance not to have been much affected by inflation:

> *Up to 1885, 500 coconuts were equal to 1 rupee. Later, the "parity" was 300. In 1901 the rate quoted in the Census of India was 100 per rupee. When it was decided after the First World War to impose an export duty on all goods exported from the islands, the exchange rate was officially fixed at 200 nuts per rupee. Subsequently the value of the rupee was reduced once more to 100 nuts, and later to 64. (Einzig, 1949, p. 112)*

Car Nicobar was a possession of British India at this time, and unlike Great Britain, that part of the Empire was toiling under a silver standard. In the second half of the 19th century, the gold-to-silver ratio expanded considerably due to the demand of gold rising and the demand of silver falling in light of the gold standards. Despite this, it seems the price of coconuts held its ground good compared to silver, which is quite remarkable considering the ease at which coconuts grew, and the many complications of getting silver up from deep mines. The main explanation of the discrepancy lies in the fact that coconuts naturally deteriorate, so that while a silver rupee physically remains the same over decades, a coconut soon enough loses all its desired properties as food and drink, and ultimately even as money. Einzig's comparison is in other words slightly skewed.

On a similar note, he ends his research of the Nicobar coconut currency by taking a further interest in this apparent lack of inflation:

> *The coconut currency is never liable to be inflated, for if there is no adequate demand for coconuts when they are ripe, then islanders just do not trouble to collect them. Nor is there any evidence that the increase in the value of coconuts from 500 to the rupee in 1885 to 48 to the rupee 40 years later—an appreciation of 900 per cent—has in any way upset the primitive economy of Nicobar. They just think in terms of coconuts, and if the rupee costs less coconuts then so much the worse for the rupee. (Einzig, 1949, p. 113)*

Einzig completely misunderstands the nature of money. Coconut money was always liable to be inflated; it just happened to be that alternatives like silver were rather unsuitable during the time period that he studied. Coconut deterioration was a cost the islanders could not escape. But even if they could, as soon as coconuts accrued a premium from them functioning as money, it would create an economic incentive for producers to plant more trees in order to increase future production. Since this was not that hard to do in the tropical climate of the islands, coconuts would never be money with adequate hardness, which is why no larger society even came close in using such money.

Finally, the Nicobar coconuts provide a good example of the futility of relying on non-monetary utility of money. It has been argued *in infinitum* that silver or gold is good money because the precious metals can also be used in industries, in jewelry, or in consumer electronics. The same argument can of course be put forward for the potential health effects and good taste of coconut milk and coconut meat. A coconut's outer layer of fiber is and has been extensively used in products such as floor mats. Yet, none of the above use cases managed to keep the coconut money on the island throne for long as soon as harder silver came into closer proximity of the people using it.

6. The 'Secret of Alchemy'

T he journey at sea proceeded, and after a brief visit to the Malay Archipelago, Battúta finally reached the Empire of the Great Khan (who at the time was Toghon Temür of the Yuan dynasty, a descendant of Genghis Khan):

> The land of China is of vast extent, and abounding in produce, fruits, grain, gold and silver. In this respect there is no country in the world that can rival it. (Battúta, 1325-1354, p. 282)

Bark of the Mulberry Tree

After speaking briefly on the agricultural produce of the land and its quality pottery, Battúta turned his attention to a phenomenon common today, but very rare in the 14th century: the use of paper-money:

> The Chinese use neither [gold] dinars nor [silver] dirhams in their commerce. All the gold and silver that comes into their country is cast by

75

them into ingots, as we have described. Their
buying and selling is carried on exclusively by
means of pieces of paper, each of the size of the
palm of the hand, and stamped with the sultan's
seal. Twenty-five of these pieces of paper are called
a balisht, which takes the place of the dinar with
us [as the unit of currency]. [...] If anyone goes to
the bazaar with a silver dirham or a dinar,
intending to buy something, no one will accept it
from him or pay any attention to him until he
changes it for balisht, and with that he may buy
what he will. (Battúta, 1325-1354, p. 284)

Similar observations had been made half a century earlier, by
Venetian explorer Marco Polo. Marco's story in China started
with his father and uncle, who after having set out from
Constantinople to Crimea reached as far as Kublai Khan's
Mongol empire in China. Impressed by the two Venetians, the
Khan had sent them back to Europe, and more specifically to the
Pope, to fetch a hundred learned Christians for the Mongol court.
With a golden tablet received from the Khan, they could pass
unmolested throughout his dominion. Upon having arrived in
Acre – then still possessed by the Crusaders – they had learned
that the Pope was dead and that no new had yet been chosen.
This prompted the two brothers to return to Venice to see to their
households, where a 15-year-old Marco awaited them and met
them for the first time. Marco joined the party that again set out
for Kublai's court.

His description of the Khan's paper money have him appear
more impressed than Battúta:

Now that I have told you in detail of the
splendour of this City of the Emperor's, I shall
proceed to tell you of the Mint which he hath in
the same city, in the which he hath his money

*coined and struck, as I shall relate to you. And in
doing so I shall make manifest to you how it is that
the Great Lord may well be able to accomplish
even much more than I have told you, or am going
to tell you, in this Book. For, tell it how I might,
you never would be satisfied that I was keeping
within truth and reason!*

*The Emperor's Mint then is in this same City
of Cambaluc [Beijing], and the way it is wrought
is such that you might say he hath the Secret of
Alchemy in perfection, and you would be right!
For he makes his money after this fashion.*

*He makes them take of the bark of a certain
tree, in fact of the Mulberry Tree, the leaves of
which are the food of the silkworms — these trees
being so numerous that whole districts are full of
them.* (Polo, The Book of Ser Marco Polo, the
Venetian Vol I, 1271-1295, p. 378)

Polo, described by translators of his documentations as generally
radiating "little or no humour or emotion" in his recounting,
clearly was astonished by the fact that Kublai Khan made money
from a tree. He would likely have been more surprised had he
known that the silk produce of the mulberry tree worms
previously had been money in China, and that even the
mulberries themselves had been money in Turkestan (Quiggin,
1949, p. 192). Henry Yule, as he translated Rustichello's notes,
commented on Polo's reaction:

*Of humour there are hardly any signs in his
Book. His almost solitary joke [...] occurs in
speaking of the Kaan's paper-money, when he
observes that Kublai might be said to have the true
Philosopher's Stone, for he made his money at*

pleasure out of the bark of Trees. (Polo, The Book
of Ser Marco Polo, the Venetian Vol I, 1271-1295,
p. cxxxiii)

Broken Promises

As with all claims of successful alchemy, this appears to have
been greatly overstated as well. Yule commented critically on the
Khan's paper money:

> *The issue of paper-money in China is at least*
> *as old as the beginning of the 9th century. In 1160*
> *the system had gone to such excess that*
> *government paper equivalent in nominal value to*
> *43,600,000 ounces of silver had been issued in six*
> *years, and there were local notes besides; so that*
> *the Empire was flooded with rapidly depreciating*
> *paper. The Kin or "Golden" Dynasty of Northern*
> *Invaders who immediately preceded the Mongols*
> *took to paper, in spite of their title, as kindly as the*
> *native sovereigns. Their notes had a course of*
> *seven years, after which new notes were issued to*
> *the holders, with a deduction of 15 per cent. [...]*

> *The Mongols commenced their issues of*
> *paper-money in 1236, long before they had*
> *transferred the seat of their government to China.*
> *Kublai made such an issue in the first year of his*
> *reign (1260), and continued to issue notes*
> *copiously till the end. In 1287 he put out a*
> *complete new currency, one note of which was to*
> *exchange against five of the previous series of*
> *equal nominal value! In both issues the paper-*
> *money was, in official valuation, only equivalent*
> *to half its nominal value in silver. The paper-*
> *money was called Chao. (Polo, The Book of Ser*

Marco Polo, the Venetian Vol I, 1271-1295, pp. 380-381)

In other words, it appears that Polo's marvels at the phenomenon of paper money were slightly premature, albeit understandable. It probably didn't occur to him to fully appreciate the danger of having the state being able to produce money at a minimal cost. The Khan's money, by design, could be mass produced to the detriment of all its holders.

In fact, such mass production may have been the very reason Kublai Khan then sat on his throne in the first place. The Chinese Song dynasty, which fell to the Mongols in the 13th century, had through paper money degraded the commercial state of their empire, and so also the defense, which caused Peter St. Onge to argue that the inflation itself was the main course of this fall:

> *This fiat-money-enabled economic stagnation and fiscal deadweight then led to proximate causes of the Song's decline: high inflation, widespread corruption, a series of aggressive wars with neighbors, and alienation of local landlords, merchants, and producers. Combined, these results facilitated what would otherwise have been an unlikely conquest by much smaller neighbors. (Onge, 2017, p. 224)*

Yule continues his more neutral take of the history of Chinese paper money:

> *To complete the history of the Chinese paper-currency so far as we can: In 1309, a new issue took place with the same provision as in Kublai's last issue, i.e. each note of the new issue was to exchange against 5 of the last of the same nominal value. And it was at the same time prescribed that the notes should exchange at par with metals,*

which of course it was beyond the power of
Government to enforce, and so the notes were
abandoned. Issues continued from time to time to
the end of the Mongol Dynasty. The paper-
currency is spoken of by Odoric (1320-30), by
Pegolotti (1330-40), and by Ibn Batuta (1348), as
still the chief, if not sole, currency of the Empire.
According to the Chinese authorities, the credit of
these issues was constantly diminishing, as 'tis
easy to suppose. But it is odd that all the Western
Travellers speak as if the notes were as good as
gold. Pegolotti, writing for mercantile men, and
from the information (as we may suppose) of
mercantile men, says explicitly that there was no
depreciation. (Polo, The Book of Ser Marco Polo,
the Venetian Vol I, 1271-1295, p. 382)

This is strange indeed. Marco Polo also corroborates Battuta's claim that notes were readily taken by merchants. The fact that not accepting them meant capital punishment might have had something to do with it. Yule also mentions that the 14th-15th century Ming dynasty that succeeded Toghon Temür's failing Yuan dynasty, made use of paper money as well, but that it only paid with notes while demanding payments in "hard cash" (meaning silver and gold). In 1448 A.D. the Chao of 1000 cash, according to Yule, was worth only 3, and the paper-money system fell into disuse.

Yule ends the explanatory note on Chinese paper money by mentioning, at that time, current developments on the subject:

Some fifteen years ago [counting from 1871]
the Imperial [Chinese] Government seems to have
been induced by the exhausted state of the
Treasury, and these large examples of the local use
of paper-currency, to consider projects for

> *resuming that system after the disuse of four*
> *centuries. A curious report by a committee of the*
> *Imperial Supreme Council, on a project for such a*
> *currency, appears among the papers published by*
> *the Russian Mission at Peking. It is unfavourable*
> *to the particular project, but we gather from other*
> *sources that the Government not long afterwards*
> *did open banks in the large cities of the Empire for*
> *the issue of a new paper currency, but that it met*
> *with bad success. At Fuchau, in 1858, I learn from*
> *one notice, the dollar was worth from 18,000 to*
> *20,000 cash in Government Bills. Dr. Rennie, in*
> *1861, speaks of the dollar at Peking as valued at*
> *15,000 and later at 25,000 paper cash. (Polo, The*
> *Book of Ser Marco Polo, the Venetian Vol II,*
> *1271-1295, pp. 382-383)*

In other words, the spectre of easy money never stopped haunting China. As Yule mentioned, four centuries of disuse was apparently enough for Chinese authorities to forget the country's bad experiences with such a system.

Yule also mentions a vague connection between Marco Polo and yet another attempt at paper-money in Persia at the time of Polo's travels. Having exhausted the Treasury in 1294 A.D., Kaikhatu Khan, on the suggestion of an innovative financial officer named Izzuddin Muzaffar, introduced a copy of the Chinese *Chao* money in the districts under his control. Even details like Chinese characters were present on the notes, as was the name *Chao* itself. Yule:

> *After the constrained use of the Chao for two*
> *or three days Tabriz was in an uproar; the markets*
> *were closed; the people rose and murdered*
> *'Izzuddin; and the whole project had to be*

81

> *abandoned. (Polo, The Book of Ser Marco Polo, the*
> *Venetian Vol I, 1271-1295, p. 384)*

These remarkable examples of economic stupidity are clear examples of the lure of *easy money*. The supposedly redeemable banknotes of the many Mongol and Chinese dynasties would ultimately fail due to the fact that the unanswerable authority, with its immense power and soldiers, had few incentives to keep the redeemability intact. Wars were costly and frequent in 13th and 14th century China, which could be what pushed the authorities to the point where they decided to print more notes than they had backing for in specie. Any initial hardness of the Khan's paper money was always artificial, and this money, like so many others, was ultimately dethroned as well.

Chinese Authoritarianism

On a related note, it is likely not a coincidence that paper money first emerged in a part of the world wrought with deep-rooted authoritarianism. Such traces could be observed by multiple medieval travelers, and not only with regards to the harsh punishment in not accepting the Khan's paper money. Various monies, like silk and wheat, had long before the Mongol Khans been forbidden as such in China (Einzig, 1949, p. 285). And as we will later see was the case with the Sultanate of Delhi, the city of Cambaluc, or "The City of the Emperor", suffered forced migrations through central planning as well, though far from as severe as its Indian counterpart. The moving of the city was mandated by Kublai Khan, on information from his astrologers that the old Cambaluc would prove rebellious and troublesome.[17] Also like in the Sultanate of Delhi, the Khan's secret police seems, according to Battúta, to have had a habit of gathering information on all foreign travelers:

---

[17] (Polo, The Book of Ser Marco Polo, the Venetian Vol I, 1271-1295, p. 331)

When I visited the sultan's city I passed with my companions through the painters' bazaar on my way to the sultan's palace. We were dressed after the `Iraqí fashion. On returning from the palace in the evening, I passed through the same bazaar, and saw my portrait and those of my companions drawn on a sheet of paper which they had affixed to the wall. Each of us set to examining the other's portrait [and found that] the likeness was perfect in every respect. I was told that the sultan had ordered them to do this, and that they had come to the palace while we were there and had been observing us and drawing our portraits without our noticing it. This is a custom of theirs, I mean making portraits of all who pass through their country. In fact they have brought this to such perfection that if a stranger commits any offence that obliges him to flee from China, they send his portrait far and wide. A search is then made for him and wheresoever the [person bearing a] resemblance to that portrait is found he is arrested. (Battúta, 1325-1354, pp. 285-286)

The surveillance extended to all the hostelries in the vast empire as well:

At every post-station in their country they have a hostelry controlled by an officer, who is stationed there with a company of horsemen and footsoldiers. After sunset or later in the evening the officer visits the hostelry with a clerk, registers the name of all travellers staying there for the night, seals up the list, and locks them into the hostelry. After sunrise he returns with his clerk, calls each person by name, and writes a detailed *description of them on the list. He then sends a man with them to conduct them to the next post-station and bring back a clearance certificate from the controller there to the effect that all these persons have arrived at the station. If the guide does not produce this document, he is held responsible for them. (Battúta, 1325-1354, p. 287)*

The Khan, at least as Polo visited the country, also imposed curfew in the cities every evening. Anyone found outside after a certain hour was arrested, according to him:

Moreover, in the middle of the city there is a great clock – that is to say, a bell – which is struck at night. And after it has struck three times no one must go out in the city, unless it be for the needs of a woman in labour, or of the sick. And those who go about on such errands are bound to carry lanterns with them. Moreover, the established guard at each gate of the city is 1000 armed men; not that you are to imagine this guard is kept up for fear of any attack, but only as a guard of honour for the Sovereign, who resides there, and to prevent thieves from doing mischief in the town. (Polo, The Book of Ser Marco Polo, the Venetian Vol I, 1271-1295, p. 332)

[…]

Guards patrol the city every night in parties of 30 or 40, looking out for any persons who may be abroad at unreasonable hours, i.e. after the great bell hath stricken thrice. If they find any such person he is immediately taken to prison, and examined next morning by the proper officers.

84

(Polo, The Book of Ser Marco Polo, the Venetian Vol I, 1271-1295, p. 368)

It is quite evident that the desire to control money stemmed from an overarching desire to have power and control over subjects, who were then ever so often, in times of war or just frivolous royal spending on palaces or harems or the like, reduced to a toiling collective of nameless serfs.

7. Sugar Money in the West

As China fell into civil war during Battúta's visit, he was strongly encouraged to leave the country. This he did, and Ibn Juzzay only briefly describes the westward route which barely touched India due to Battúta's fear of the wrathful Sultan, in whose employment he at least nominally still was. It was during this time that the Bubonic Plague reached Persia and Syria through caravansaries, and Cairo, Constantinople and other European cities through rat-infested ships. Battúta found himself in the middle of this spread and reported incredible death tolls:

> *Early in June we heard at Aleppo that the plague had broken out at Gaza, and that the number of deaths there reached over a thousand per day. On traveling to Hims I found that the plague had broken out there: about three hundred persons died of it on the day I arrived. So I went to Damascus, and arrived there on a Thursday. The inhabitants had been fasting for three days; on the Friday they went out to the mosque of the*

> *Footprints, as we have related in the first book,*
> *and God eased them of the plague. The number of*
> *deaths among them reached a maximum of 2,400*
> *a day. (Battúta, 1325-1354, p. 305)*

Upon reaching Hormuz he met a fellow countryman who came
with more sad news – this time about the homeland:

> *I met there a man from Morocco, who*
> *informed me of the disaster at Tarifa, and of the*
> *capture of al-Khadrá [Algeciras] by the Christians*
> *– may God repair the breach that Islám has*
> *suffered thereby! (Battúta, 1325-1354, p. 303)*

The battle was one of the culminating events in a conflict that
Marinid sultan Abu al-Hasan 'Ali of Morocco had been drawn
into by the Sultanate of Granada. With a goal to help the pressed
neighboring Muslim state, and establish a Marinid power base in
the Iberian Peninsula, Abu al-Hasan 'Ali had agreed to send both
troops and ships. But with the help of Portuguese knights, the
Castilians managed to route the Moroccans, who consequently
had to abandon the campaign. The conflict may be counted as a
part of a larger game: the Reconquista, or the supposed
reclaiming of Iberian lands by Christians.

Expulsion of the Sugar Masters

Battúta became part of this game as soon as he reached his
hometown Tangier. Crossing the seas from Ceuta to Andalusia,
he felt indebted to join in "the *jihád* and the defense of the
frontier". After meeting his cousin, the *qádí* of Ronda, Battúta
reached Marbella, where the enemy kept dangerously close.
Meeting a group of twelve riders about to set out for Malaga,
Battúta hesitated to join them, which he later thanked God for
upon learning one of them was killed while ten others were
captured. It appears that the Christians only halted their

advances when the Castilian King Alfonso XI died of the plague that year – a cause for some dark irony as while the plague killed Battúta's own mother, it may also have saved his life in that conflict. He could safely head back to Morocco to prepare for his final journey.

The Reconquista attracted both Muslims like Battúta, and Christian volunteers from all over Europe. It ended in 1492 A.D., when the last defenses of Granada finally fell. As part of the Spanish Inquisition, Spain's large Jewish and Muslim populations were either expelled or converted; many found refuge in the Ottoman Empire. The Jews definitively had to leave as a result of the 1492 Alhambra Decree, but the Muslims only felt the same urgency after rebelling in light of widespread forced conversion policies and torture. All this caused widespread anger among Muslim states, and prompted the Ottoman Sultan Bayezid II to ridicule Ferdinand II and Isabella I's conduct, stating to his courtiers "You venture to call Ferdinand a wise ruler, he who has impoverished his own country and enriched mine!" (Singer, 1902, p. 460). Bayecid II's navy shipped families to Ottoman provinces, leaving large, depopulated areas behind. One of many industries that suffered consequences was the production of sugar – something which had monetary repercussions many years later, as we soon shall see.

A historical study on sugar has been conducted and summarized by Stuart B. Schwartz and some fellow sugar historians in *Tropical Babylons: Sugar and the Making of the Atlantic World, 1450-1680*. Schwartz, mostly focusing on the crop itself and how it spread, only touches on the subject of commodity money in the Appendix of his book.

Sugar cane plantations were introduced to the West Indies in the 16th century by Spanish and Portuguese colonists, who already grew the commodity in the Mediterranean, on Madeira, and on the Canaries. The sugar crops had been introduced to various parts of Europe by Muslims conquering the Iberian Peninsula, and later by crusading Christians who had found the produce in the Levant. Fetching a high price on the open market, the crop interested noblemen as well as merchant houses. Yet, growing it in Iberia was not always easy. Producing sugar demanded a lot of water, and there were often opposition to diverting the flow of rivers to sugar mills to the detriment of other, already established mills. Something that further destroyed the sugar production in Iberia was exactly the mentioned expulsion of the Moors and later Moriscos– all having made up a major part of both work force and know-how.

Caribbean Plantations

The high price instead lead to the west-ward expansion of sugar plantations on islands in the eastern Atlantic, where the crop grew with more ease than in the settlers' homelands. Española (modern day Haiti and Dominican Republic) came to be the early powerhouse of Caribbean sugar production after settlers found cultivation efforts highly successful there. After the gold industry on the island faltered in the beginning of the 16th century due to the near annihilation of indigenous labor, colonists further shifted focus to the crop instead. The ability of the crop to grow on the island had first been verified when Columbus brought cane cuttings from Madeira, and soon enough sugar plantations and mills were sprawling all over the Caribbean.

As sugarcane crops, once cut, had to be processed within 48 hours lest the juice inside dried, the plantations had not only agrarian but industrial elements to them as well. The nature of the whole production process (planting, growing, cutting, milling, cooking, crystallizing, packing and shipping) made for factory-like conditions in which the workforce, often made up of slaves, was heavily regimented. A certain Father António Vieira, who visited a Jesuit-owned plantation in Brazil, noted:

> *People the color of the very night, working*
> *briskly and moaning at the same time without a*
> *moment of peace and rest, whoever sees all the*
> *confused and noisy machinery and apparatus of*
> *this Babylon, even if they have seen Mt. Etnas and*
> *Vesuvius will say that this indeed is the image of*
> *Hell. (Schwartz, 2004, p. 3)*

The heavy capital requirement of the industry likely caused lagging effects on where and how it spread. Barbados was one example of a late adopter. Around 1640, its economy was in trouble after the tobacco and cotton industries on the island failed to be competitive (especially as its tobacco was deemed inferior to for example Virginian one). British colonists thus appear to, partially with investment and support from the Dutch, have pivoted to establishing a sugar economy instead. Bringing in thousands of slaves from Africa, other local commercial activities were slowly crowded out while sugar expanded to become by far the largest export of the island. One British planter noted:

> *Men are so intent upon planting sugar that*
> *they rather buy food at very dear rates than*
> *produce it by labor, so infinite is the profits of*
> *sugar works after once accomplished. (Schwartz,*
> *2004, p. 290)*

The importance of sugar to the population of Barbados, mixed with other external factors, was enough cause for a new monetary system to evolve. Having no mint themselves, the island population had for quite some time used both cotton, tobacco and foreign silver coins as money. British pounds sterling were severely lacking in the region due to Britain's strict colonial policy of not allowing its silver coins to flow out to the colonies as it felt the relationship ought to be the opposite. In exchange for British protection and specific goods, British authorities argued, the job of its colonies was to provide Britain with cheap commodities as well as to develop markets for its mercantile expansion. The colonists, in other words, had the same problem of chronic silver coin shortages as their North American counterparts, and had to be inventive around unconventional forms of money to facilitate economic exchange. Paul Einzig commented on the situation as well:

> *Foreign merchants reproached the Islanders for having no money except brown sugar. Lord (Francis) Willoughby of Parham stated in 1664 that "the current medium on the Island consisted of goods for they had no money." (Einzig, 1949, p. 300)*

Being commonly used is not the main requirement for a commodity money to evolve. Sugar was often fungible, highly divisible, relatively easy to transport, could be packaged in a standardized way, and was not very perishable if kept away from humidity. The island supply of it was, at least initially, under relative control, and with Britain not exporting its silver coins there, it was enough for this new money to evolve.

And so the Barbados legislature passed several new laws from 1640 and onward, that made sugar legal tender. Some evidence suggests that an initial rate of around 6 pence of what was called Barbados pound sterling was pegged to one pound of sugar. Despite its name, this Barbados money had nothing to do with specie but was rather part of an extensive bookkeeping system – a money of account– the British used for some of its colonies. This explains why the exchange rate of Barbados pound sterling to British pound sterling for a long time was close to at par. Due to the bookkeeping system, the colonists only quoted prices in that money, but settled trades in commodity money like sugar. The official exchange rate to sugar fell to 3 pence per pound in 1652, and to 2 pence per pound in the end of that decade. In the 1660's, the fixed exchange rate dropped to 1.5 pence per pound of sugar, after which the British to some degree started to monetize the island with silver and took the true significance out of sugar as money there. (Schwartz, 2004, p. 331)

This constant appreciation of the Barbados pound sterling should be viewed in the light of it being an artificial byproduct from Britain's monetary bookkeeping system, and from the fact that the Brits had silver money. As the sugar industry productivity and size increased on Barbados (and on other islands for that matter), cheaper sugar could be used to exchange for goods still quoted in Barbados pound sterling at a, to sugar, fixed exchange rate. One pound of sugar could initially make a merchant legally entitled to settle a trade- or tax bill worth 6 pence of Barbados pound sterling, meaning approximately 6 pence of British pound sterling. It is likely that the colonial administration, as was the case in North America, directly or indirectly provided much of the slaves and goods Barbados needed to produce all its sugar, while at the same time keeping the British pound sterling out. It is easy to understand then, how simple it must have been for the administration to effectively devalue sugar money so that plantation owners, despite increasing productivity, retained virtually the same purchasing power.

In conclusion, the Barbados case was more complicated than when only the free market is involved in pinning hard and easy monies against each other until one breaks. The complication came from the British power over the island. But it still goes to show that Barbados merchants or planters that (perhaps involuntarily) saved and traded in sugar money would end up seeing a continuous depreciation hurting their savings. The depreciation of course came from the ease of which sugar production could increase should the price of sugar go up. Colonists on Barbados, trapped under a combination of a lack of monetary hardness and British authoritarianism, had no choice but to accept inflation or try to acquire foreign silver at a large premium.

8. Mountains, Deserts and Oceans of Salt

Battúta, now home from Spain, eventually ventured eastward from Marrakesh towards Sijilmása, a small town on the northern outskirts of the vast and deadly Saharan Desert. There he acquired enough provisions for a long, hot journey south towards Tagházá, which was situated by the southernmost extremity of the sand dunes. That arduous journey took him and his party 25 full days, and as they arrived, Battúta was quick to notice the inhabitants lived off salt production:

> *There are no trees there, nothing but sand. In the sand is a salt mine; they dig for the salt, and find it in thick slabs, lying on top of the other, as though they had been tool-squared and laid under the surface of the earth. A camel will carry two of these slabs. No one lives at Tagházá except the slaves of the Massúfa tribe, who dig for the salt; they subsist on dates imported from Dar'a and*

> *Sijilmása, camels' flesh, and millet imported from the [land of the Blacks]. The [blacks] come up from their country and take away the salt from there. At Iwálátan a load of salt brings eight to ten mithqals; in the town of Málli it sells for twenty to thirty, and sometimes as much as forty. The [blacks] use salt as a medium of exchange, just as gold and silver is used [elsewhere]; they cut it up into pieces and buy and sell with it. The business done at Tagházá, for all its meaness, amounts to an enormous figure in terms of hundredweights of gold-dust. (Battúta, 1325-1354, pp. 317-318)*

Salt Scarcities

Salt proves yet one additional example of how a commodity can first emerge and then get dethroned as money; this consequently helps us better understand the monetary frameworks discussed earlier. Historically, salt was often used to prolong the lifespan of food products, and so functioned as a vital hedge against periods of hunger. This function, among others, had it traded against other goods on marketplaces all over the world, across all ages. But only at a few of these markets did it function as money. One of those was observed by Marco Polo as he traveled the lands of Kublai Khan:

> *They [the Tibetans] have none of the Great Kaan's paper money, but use salt instead of money. (Polo, The Book of Ser Marco Polo, the Venetian Vol II, 1271-1295, p. 29)*

Further east, in the province of Caindu (modern-day Xichang), he also reported on salt money. Curiously, that money seems to have functioned in parallel with early stages of coinage – a phenomenon which as we have seen appears to have been rather common:

> *The money matters of the people are conducted in this way. They have gold in rods which they weigh, and they reckon its value by its weight in saggi, but they have no coined money. Their small change again is made in this way. They have salt which they boil and set in mould, and every piece from the mould weights about half a pound. Now, 80 moulds of this salt are worth one saggio of fine gold, which is a weight so called. So this salt serves them for small change. (Polo, The Book of Ser Marco Polo, the Venetian Vol II, 1271-1295, p. 35)*

Henry Yule, the translator of the transcribed recounts of Polo's travels, refers to more modern sources that corroborated the above. Salt brought to wild mountain populations in the region could fetch as high a price as 40 pieces of salt moulds per saggio of gold, indicating local gold abundances and salt scarcities. Similar observations of large geographical price differences were made by Portuguese missionary Francisco Álvares, in his description of Ethiopia a few centuries later:

> *There is in it [the land] the best thing there is in Ethiopia, that is the salt, which in all the country is current as money, both in the kingdoms and dominions of the Prester and in the kingdoms of the Moors and Gentiles, and they say that it goes as far as Manicongo. [...] They say that in the place where the salt is collected a hundred and twenty or a hundred and thirty stones are worth a drachm [...]. Then, at a market which is in our road, at a town named Corcora, which is about a day's journey from the place where the salt is got, it already is worth five or six stones less, and so it goes on diminishing from market to*

> *market. When it arrives at court, six or seven*
> *stones are worth a drachm; I have seen them at*
> *five to the drachm when it was winter. (Álvares,*
> *1540, pp. 98-99)*

So, here we have a few examples of salt being used as money, in different places on Earth and across different time periods. The reason for all of them was simple: temporarily superior saleableness. Salt, being highly saleable across scales and relatively saleable across space, could only become money where it was also saleable across time. This meant that salt became money where it was relatively scarce in relation to existing quantities, and salt was relatively scarce in relation to existing quantities only where it was relatively hard to produce or transport. In Yule's annotations, he briefly mentions a note from a certain M. Francis Garnier that shows the essence of this dynamic:

> *Salt currency has a very wide diffusion from*
> *Muang Yong to Sheu-pin. In the Shan markets,*
> *especially within the limits named, all purchases*
> *are made with salt. At Seumao and Pouheul,*
> *silver, weighed and cut in small pieces, is in our*
> *day tending to drive out the custom; but in former*
> *days it must have been universal in the tract of*
> *which I am speaking. The salt itself, prime*
> *necessity that it is, has there to be extracted by*
> *condensation from saline springs of great depth, a*
> *very difficult affair. The operation consumes*
> *enormous quantities of fuel, and to this is partly*
> *due the denudation of the country. (Polo, The*
> *Book of Ser Marco Polo, the Venetian Vol II,*
> *1271-1295, p. 37)*

Salt, in other words, naturally had a higher likelihood to evolve as money only where its stock-to-flow ratio could remain high in the face of price increases; no producer could quickly flood the market with it, which would have caused immediate dilution of its value. In addition to the instances of salt money discussed above, it emerged also in New Guinea, Borneo, the Alu islands, Zimmé, Sema Nagas, Guely and Zambia.[18]

'Supplying the World to the End of Time'

Had certain components of saleableness been drastically different, it is easy to imagine what quickly would have happened to these salt-based monetary systems. From western China stretched the Silk Road – a heavily trafficked trade network reaching as far as the Mediterranean. Maybe unbeknownst to many of its travelers, it circumvented the Dasht-e Kavir, or the Great Salt Desert, in what today is Iran. Being extremely inhospitable, salt mining was likely possible anyway, especially with the use of slaves. In another Persian province that Marco Polo traversed, salt was so abundant that the region was described as "a country divided into deserts that are salt, and deserts that are not salt"[19]. Had these salt deposits been more easily exploitable and not situated in the middle of vast deserts, any salt money within caravan reach would have, over time, been demonetized. Large scale salt production did in fact sometimes occur in proximity to the salt-money societies, but it is unclear to what extent this production caused demonetization in the end. Marco Polo

> *A great amount of salt also is made here [Coiganju, or Hwai-Ngan-Chau], furnishing some forty other cities with that article, and bringing in a great revenue to the Great Kaan [...].*

---

[18] (Einzig, 1949)

[19] (Polo, The Book of Ser Marco Polo, the Venetian Vol I, 1271-1295, p. 120)

(Polo, The Book of Ser Marco Polo, the Venetian Vol II, 1271-1295, p. 114)

At every place between the sea and the city [Tiju] salt is made in great quantities. And there is a rich and noble city called Tinju, at which there is produced enough to supply the whole province [...]. (Polo, The Book of Ser Marco Polo, the Venetian Vol II, 1271-1295, p. 116)

Polo even mentions whole mountains of salt in Taican – modern day Kunduz in Afghanistan – which is quite far from China's and Tibet's salt money markets, but may still have contributed considerably to excessive new supply in the end:

After those twelve days' journey you come to a fortified place called Taican, where there is a great corn market. It is a fine place, and the mountains that you see towards the south are all composed of salt. People from all the countries round, to some thirty days' journey, come to fetch this salt, which is the best in the world, and is so hard that it can only be broken with iron picks. 'Tis in such abundance that it would supply the whole world to the end of time. (Polo, The Book of Ser Marco Polo, the Venetian Vol I, 1271-1295, p. 145)

And finally, we have one important account from Polo while visiting Hangzhou in eastern China:

Now I will tell you about the great revenue which the Great Khaan draweth every year from the said city of Kinsay and its territory, which forms a ninth part of the whole country of Manzi. First there is the salt, which brings in a great revenue. For it produces every year, in round numbers, fourscore tomans of gold; and the toman is worth 70,000 saggi of gold, so that the total value of the fourscore tomans will be five millions and six hundred thousand saggi of gold, each saggio being worth more than a gold florin or ducat; in sooth, a vast sum of money! [This province, you see, adjoins the ocean, on the shores of which are many lagoons or salt marches, in which the sea-water dries up during the summer time; and thence they extract such a quantity of salt as suffices for the supply of five of the kingdoms of Manzi besides this one.] (Polo, The Book of Ser Marco Polo, the Venetian Vol II, 1271-1295, p. 171)

As soon as the owners of the salt deserts, the salt mountains and the salt lagoons were to get word of monetary systems based on that good, and if these monetary systems were geographically close enough for salt's physical properties over time and space to warrant action, we can be sure that attention quickly would have turned to the opportunity on how to extract the white mineral in the greatest quantities imaginable, causing its rapid depreciation and dethronement everywhere.

9. Cloth Money in Africa

Battúta traveled the provinces of the Empire of Mali during the year 1352 A.D. As with many of his trips, the journey was dangerous even after having crossed the Sahara due to water still being scarce. He and his caravan passed at least one traveler dead from thirst, and Battúta speaks about desert demons causing people to lose their orientation. Upon reaching Iwálátan (Oualata), Battúta stayed there for fifty days and observed, among other things, the widespread use of fine Egyptian fabrics (Battúta, 1325-1354, p. 320).

Money of the Caravans

He also met Mansá Sulaymán, the Sultan of Mali and brother of the late and admired Mansa Musa. Perhaps due to having heard of Mansa Musa's riches, Battúta, more demanding now in older age, was highly disappointed with the gifts he received by the current sultan. After visiting the capital Timbuktu, and the city of Gogo, he set out towards Tagaddá with a large caravan. Tagaddá is described as an important trading town with regards to the Egyptian fabric already mentioned. It was in this town that Battúta received a command from the Sultan of Morocco to return home at once, and so he started preparations for his journey north across the desert, and stocked up on an interesting good:

> *I kissed the order and conformed to its instructions. I bought two riding-camels for thirty-seven and a third mithqáls and prepared for the journey to Tawát. I took with me provisions for seventy days, for there is no corn to be had between Tagaddá and Tawát, only fleshmeat, milk and butter, which are paid for with pieces of cloth. (Battúta, 1325-1354, p. 337)*

This would not be the first time he and his companions would have to pay with cloths. When Battúta and a large number of other pilgrims much earlier crossed the Arabian Desert in a north-eastern direction, they had an encounter with Bedouins – an event not that interesting per se, if it wasn't for the fact that those Bedouins as well had demanded to be paid in that good:

> *The Badawin [Bedouins] of that district [Samira] come here with sheep, melted butter, and milk, which they sell to the pilgrims for pieces of coarse cotton cloth. That is the only thing they will take in exchange. (Battúta, 1325-1354, p. 79)*

It should be added that the pilgrims from Mecca of course had access to gold dinars and silver dirhams, and yet it was cotton cloth money that the nomads demanded. Had history provided us with only these indication of the use of cotton cloth money, one could arguably be forgiven to brush the subject aside. But this is not the case. Battúta heard of a similar phenomenon upon traveling Yemen, where Arab brigands often demanded cloths in exchange for not occupying the water supply infrastructure of various cities (Battúta, 1325-1354, pp. 109-110). In the interior of parts of East Africa, cloths were used by trade caravans to bribe their way through local chiefdoms (Pallaver, 2009, p. 21). Silk was used as money in Ancient China, resulting in etymological curiosities like the word *pu*, meaning "cloth", eventually assuming the meaning of "money" (Einzig, 1949, p. 256), and in Roman times, silk cloth was sometimes estimated to be worth its weight in gold in the west (Quiggin, 1949, p. 221). With all that said, little did Battúta know that much of the cloth trade he observed in Mali would be greatly disrupted for monetary reasons a century or so later – with the arrival of Portuguese settlers.

The New Cloth Traders

As part of its "Money in Africa"-project, the British Museum has a research publication by Carlos. F. Liberato, who provides further evidence of long-lasting systems of cloth money in West Africa. The 15th to 18th century European –mainly Portuguese– meddling in the Guiné region initially makes most people think of the slave trade, and the trade in human beings was of course pivotal there. But seldom is it discussed what the Europeans used to actually pay for their cargo. They, like Battúta and the members of his caravan, used cloth as money, not for a limited period of time, but over centuries. Interestingly, the cloth money native to Africa was sometimes in mock, unusable condition since it was used only in economic exchange, not as clothes or garment (Quiggin, 1949, p. 56).

To understand the new influx of cloths, we have to go west, not only to the coast, but further. Cape Verde is an archipelago in the Atlantic Ocean, west of what today is Senegal. Portuguese explorers found the uninhabited islands in the 15th century and decided to colonize them. As it were, it turned out cotton could grow in some of the more rain-heavy areas, which, given the landscape of Guiné in the centuries thereafter, incidentally made the islands a convenient base for money production. Alvise Cadamosto, who visited the region in 1455 and 1456, was one of the first Europeans to document the fact that cotton was already grown and cultivated on the African mainland by locals (Liberato, 2009, p. 12). The Portuguese, quick to notice how relatively valuable cotton cloth strips were for the coastal inhabitants of upper Guiné, proceeded with setting up cotton plantations themselves around their newly claimed settlements.

As early as the 16th century, cloth strips had evolved as a well-established form of money in Senegambia, by the coast as well as further inland. As has been discussed, the area had important cultural and historical ties with the cotton cloths introduced over the past centuries by Muslim traders from north of Sahara. Even on Cape Verde the *barafula* (cloth strips sewn together) became the standard currency in which taxes, as well as soldier wages were paid. Despite cloths being produced locally by African tribes as well, the Portuguese were more efficient, which led to a profitable but perverse slave supply chain to Cape Verde, de facto financed by money which the slaves themselves cultivated on the island plantations. Liberato quotes Scottish historian Christopher Fyfe, who described this ecosystem in his writings:

> *Some of the slaves were weavers by profession, and wove the cotton into country cloths as they had done on the mainland. New elaborate patterns of North African type were introduced, and from the middle of the 16th century Cape Verde panos [cloth strips] were regularly exported to Guiné to be exchanged for slaves. As elsewhere in West Africa, European traders were forced to adopt African methods of accounting, and panos became recognized as units of account, just as bars and cowries were in other regions. (Liberato, 2009, p. 9)*

To strike a balance between standardization and different denominations, the Cape Verde *panos* initially came in three broad categories: *grossos* (rough), *ricos* (intricate), and *tecido fino* (delicate) fabric. It is easy to see the conceptual similarity to how coinage historically often was minted (copper, silver and gold). Despite these standardization efforts, Portuguese civil and military officials operating at various African trading posts often opposed the use of cloths as money. They had to make do, because only in 1864 did Portuguese overseas territories get an official provincial currency with the help of the Banco Nacional Ultramarino (Liberato, 2009, p. 12).

Liberato continues by mentioning that the *panos* circulating in the Rivers of Guiné fetched a value surpassing the level that could be derived from their practicality and immediate consumption, which is fully in line with the monetary theory discussed in this book. A widespread use of *panos* as a shroud for funeral corpses probably exacerbated this property. The more important the deceased, the more *panos* were used in the burial gathering, which meant the cloth strips were functioning as a public show of wealth and status. Further corroboration on the monetary properties of cloth strips came, as presented by Liberato, from a certain Francisco de Andrade in 1582:

> *[...] nothing is traded [a long the Nuno River] other than loaves of dye, like sweet bread, that are then loaded on ships that go to the São Domingos River [Cacheu], to be used by the [natives] to color their cloth black so it [the dyed cloth] can be used as money all along the other Rivers of Guiné. (Liberato, 2009, p. 12)*

Occasionally, certain slave trades could not be made without the use of these Cape Verdean cloth strips, and with this exclusivity came power. The monopoly-like situation caused Portuguese authorities to outlaw the sale of *panos* to other ships, with the very real warning of capital punishment if unheeded. This is remarkably similar to the Venetian authorities banning the export of glass bead production know-how. Yet, the islanders often sold the cloth strips to Dutch, British or French captains anyway, who then could use them to acquire slaves for their colonies.

Finally, Paul Einzig has found accounts on cotton cloth money in Guinea as well, before it was disrupted:

> *Above all, guinea cloth, as its name implies, was extensively employed as currency in Guinea. It is through the ports of Guinea that this currency penetrated into the interior to become one of the most important currencies for a long period over a vast territory of Africa. It remained a standard of value long after it ceased to be a medium of exchange. (Einzig, 1949, p. 155)*

Mass Production

In the 18th century, the Grão Pará and Maranhão Company was founded to facilitate trade between Portugal, West Africa, and the Portuguese colonies in South America. It established a state-sponsored monopoly on the production of *panos*, meaning all producers on Cape Verde had to supply the company's warehouses on the islands, from where cloths were shipped to the trading posts. Even then, hundreds of years after the first Portuguese started using cloth strips as currency when bartering with the West Africans, did the *panos* function as money. The company collected taxes and fees in *panos*, meaning it was legal tender at the time. Its monopoly also made it a large facilitator of slave trades. Not only did the semi-private Grão Pará and Maranhão Company have the right to collect taxes, it was given the right to organize and station soldiers as well–something that of course is remarkable in today's standard.

The company continued the islands' export to the West African tribes for decades. Not until later in the 18th century, when the French introduced even cheaper Indian-woven cloth strips from Pondichéry, did the Portuguese *panos* face true competition. Soon enough, American cotton reached the region as well. These are yet other examples of production- and transportation efficiencies causing monetary inflation, and it is easy to imagine Portuguese and African cloth producers bitterly cursing the French and American dilution of what was not just a commodity, but money. Certain tribal chiefs even took to the desperate method of banning, on pain of death, their subjects from wearing European cloths (Quiggin, 1949, p. 58). These dilution waves were of course inevitable, as was the one the Portuguese initially let loose on to the region. The fact that any increase in the price of cotton cloths would lead to a larger number as well as expanding cotton plantations and textile workshops, put a severe dent in the cotton cloth money's capability of defending such a price increase. And with expanding trade networks, such added production could even profitably occur on the other side of the planet, where technological advancements stemming from the Industrial Revolution had cut production costs considerably. This is what characterizes easy money, whereas with hard money, producers would struggle mightily with increased production quantities despite the increase in demand and price.

It is worth adding that while Portuguese families or companies using this fundamentally inflationary money very well could see inter-generational wealth decrease, the situation was obviously worse for the Africans. The realization is sobering; Africans experienced some of the worst possible outcomes imaginable from the fact that their own, easy money could be mass produced by the northern foreigners.

10. Muslim Copper and Heathen Gold

Before Battúta finishes his long journey, it is worth discussing a phenomenon he observed while still in Mali – in fact, the end-phase of the very dynamics that slowly took the world from primitive monies, to silver- and gold coinage. His observations intertwine with some interesting archeological findings on money in the area, described and summarized by Laurence Garenne-Marot on behalf of the British Museum[20].

Useless Metals in Kumbi Saleh

Garenne-Marot uses both translated writings as well as other evidence to piece together the monetary systems of the Sahelian kingdoms, meaning the pre-medieval Ghana Empire and its geographical successor that Battúta traversed – the Mali Empire.

---

[20] (Garenne-Marot, 2009)

His short essay interestingly also starts off by quoting Battúta, as we by now should have gotten used to:

> The houses at Tagaddá are built of red stone, and its water run by the copper mines, so that both its colour and taste are affected. There are no grain crops there except a little wheat, which is consumed by merchants and strangers. The inhabitants of Tagaddá have no occupation except trade. They travel to Egypt every year, and import quantities of all the fine fabrics to be had there and of other Egyptian wares. (Battúta, 1325-1354, p. 335)

Later, Battúta added:

> The copper mine is in the outskirts of Tagaddá. They dig the ore out of the ground, bring it to the town, and cast it in their houses. This work is done by their male and female slaves. When they obtain the red copper, they make it into bars a span and a half in length, some thin and others thick. The thick bars are sold at the rate of four hundred for a mithqal of gold, and the thin at the rate six or seven hundred to the mithqal. They serve also as a medium of exchange; with the thin bars they buy meat and firewood, with the thick, slaves, male and female, millet, butter and wheat. The copper is exported from Tagaddá to the town of Kúbar, in the regions of the heathens, to Zagháy, and to the country of Barnú, which is forty days' journey from Tagaddá. (Battúta, 1325-1354, p. 336)

In other words, it appears that he had stumbled upon a copper based monetary system, with standardization efforts in terms of

109

divisibility and weight (*mithqal*) of the minted copper bars, or rods.

Some interesting archaeological findings, referenced by Garenne-Marot, and corroborating the use of copper money, were provided by Frenchmen R. Mauny and P. Thomassey, in 1949-1951. They dug up standardized copper bars in the old Muslim merchant quarter of Kumbi Saleh – a town that was previously the capital of the vanished Ghana Empire and that had conducted a lucrative trans-Saharan trade with the Berbers and Arabs in the north. These copper bars likely functioned as money, and were much older than those observed by Battúta in Tagaddá further east. One essential observation of the archaeological findings was that some of the copper bars had been diluted with lead, which meant they likely lost much of their workable use as consumable items. The implication is that as money, it didn't matter much that the metal could not be re-smelted and consumed for non-monetary purposes.

Relentless Waves of Copper

Far northwest of Kumbi Saleh lay the town of Tegdaoust– another end point of one of the many north-south trans-Saharan trade routes. New excavations during the 1960's and 70's gave a pretty clear view that copper money production occurred in the town's workshops at a time prior to Battúta's Mali expedition. Garenne-Marot argues that not only did these workshops smelt local copper ore to trade the metal with gold in the more copper-sparse parts outside the kingdom; the merchants and metal workers of the city were smart enough to likely import relatively cheap copper and brass from north of Sahara. Some evidence of this could be seen in the finding of a large number of copper bars buried in a sand dune in the Majâbat al-Koubrâ, the most arid part of Mauritanian Sahara. That excavation point was on a trade route to Tegdaoust, and as the bars consisted not of unalloyed copper, but of brass (copper with high zinc content), it became clear that they were produced outside of Ghana/Mali (probably, according to Garenne-Marot, the mines of the Sus and Daï valleys in present day Morocco). What likely happened was that these long brass bars were used in Tegdaoust workshops to dilute the locally produced and more expensive copper, without drastically altering the color of the metal. From coming in long shapes, formed to fit being carried by camels over a long distance, they were melted, blended and formed in smaller shapes to fit donkeys that carried them south to the gold-rich areas of modern-day Guinea. Even Battúta mentioned the "heathen gold" in passing:

> Sultan Mansá Sulaymán was visited by a
> party of these [black] cannibals, including one of
> their amírs. They have a custom of wearing in
> their ears large pendants, each pendant having an
> opening of half a span. They wrap themselves in
> silk mantles, and in their country is a gold mine.
> (Battúta, 1325-1354, p. 332)

Garenne-Marot later speculates that, following disastrous raids on Tegdaoust, the north-south supply lines as well as copper money production shifted east towards Kumbi Saleh – something which might explain the relatively large number of small copper bars in that town stemming from a period after the raids.

The way some of the monetary flows in the area worked is now becoming clearer. Although gold was relatively prevalent all over Muslim West Africa, as well as in the North African sultanates, it was still of course highly valuable due to functioning as money. Mansa Musa's boastful account of incredible copper-to-gold exchange ratios in certain non-Muslim areas (corroborated by his almost proverbial wealth), combined with the copper- and brass production in the Empires of Ghana, Mali and in North Africa, made for an obvious result: Muslim merchants bought copper locally as well as imported copper and brass in order to export it to the gold producing tribes. As copper ore in a large enough geographical area is far easier to acquire than gold ore, this ultimately made it relatively simple to supply the south with the large amount of copper it so highly desired, and take locally abundant gold in exchange. Consequently, the gold-rich tribes were flooded with the (often diluted) corrosion prone metal, which in the end might have hurt its saleableness to a degree where gold slowly became ever more appreciated. That would have been an example of Thier's Law in action: bad copper money was ultimately driven out in favor of good gold money due to incessant monetary inflation.

Garenne-Marot argues in his essay that the considerable geographical differences with regards to copper-to-gold exchange ratios may also have had a cultural basis. In that case, it may be provided as an example where money as a social or cultural phenomenon can be wiped out anyway in the face of economic reality, meaning a relative abundance. And so, we can with this chapter conclude that the proposed Mengerian dynamics of money are very real, and had important repercussions on many societies and nations. One might even claim that these monetary dynamics strongly shaped history. Relative scarcities and abundances combined with ever larger trade networks and differences in technological advancement caused hundreds of monies to become mainly two: gold and silver – not by collective choice or convention, but by the actions of individuals trying to escape saleableness-related costs, including monetary inflation.

The story of money, however, does not end here. Gold-, silver- and other coinage had various problems of their own, which Battúta also sometimes observed. We will soon embark on his journey again, exploring the weaknesses and curiosities of metallic money.

Vol II: Metallic Money

Although the journey in the footsteps of both Ibn Battúta and of primitive monies now might be over, there is still a large body of monetary history left to consider, and it mainly concerns the acts of either debasing metallic coinage by adding a metal less valued than current coin contents, or tinkering with other physical properties like weights, sizes and shapes. Two common examples would be the blending of copper into silver coins, or the blending of silver into gold coins. Ibn Battúta seldom appears to have felt the need to comment much on the metal-based monetary systems that he also had to interact with, likely because he saw such systems as the standard of the more advanced economies that he was used to (the Marinid Sultanate utilized gold dinars and silver dirhams). There is however much to be said about this late stage of monetary development and evolution, which also directly has to do with the saleableness of money.

Primitive monies cannot strictly be said to have been debased in the same sense as metallic coinage often were debased over the centuries. While the effect in the end was strikingly similar – a loss of purchasing power per monetary unit – the way in which this effect came about differed and was often related to centralized power. It is more correct to attribute the many failures of primitive money to dilution caused by a natural state of abundance of the specific goods used as media of exchange. The failure of debased metallic coinage can rather be attributed to short-sighted economic incentives by powerful kings, sultans and emperors, because it was often in their power to enforce the acts of debasement even for individuals holding older, pure gold or silver coins. But physical force was not always involved, and this has caused some confusion. Attempts have been made in establishing how exactly the mints in medieval Europe lured vast amounts of purer bullion or coins for minting or re-minting, and multiple theories have been put forward. Rolnick, Velde, and Weber, in *The Debasement Puzzle: An Essay on Medieval Monetary History*[21] struggle with this apparent paradox.

It is clear that the threat of legal and physical force often accompanied debasements. First of all, owed taxes could easily be defined in the amount of pure silver or gold, or in a specific coin issue, while payments by the state could be made in newer, debased money. This is something which occurred in the Byzantine Empire[22]. The result would be that, while certain subjects received their contracted income in debased money, they still had to pay their lords with older, non-debased equivalents. And even if they paid nothing to the state, as was the case for contracted soldiers, debased payments obviously eased the state's burden of expense while lowering the purchasing power of the soldiers with an equal amount. This phenomenon was documented in Mamluk Egypt in the 16th century[23]. Another dynamic of debasements which was useful for the state was the impact on credit. An act of debasement in the form of diluting precious metal content, or shrinking the total weight of a coin issue, often had a direct effect on the money owed to other parties since the debt contracts not always specified coinage purity and weight. Loans that the state took could sometimes demand mandatory compliance, as seen in England under Henry VIII.

But interestingly, the mints also attracted bullion voluntarily with the Cantillonic lure of a somewhat higher purchasing

---

[21] (Rolnick, Velde, & Weber, 1996)

[22] (Finlay, History of the Byzantine and Greek empires, from DCCXVI to MLVII., 1853, p. 389)

[23] (Ayalon, 1958, p. 258)

power, before the general populace could properly assess the new coins according to their actual size, weight or content. In other words, privately owned bullion and old coins found their way to the mints if promised a share in the seigniorage. Evidence of such reasoning can be found in the Rolls of Parliament in England[24]. Often owing to the widespread confusions of war, inflation hid in plain sight of disturbed production and trade, and this just enhanced the debasement opportunities. So to conclude, all of the above methods were at times evidently profitable for many medieval rulers, which is why the fields of archaeology and numismatics provide example after example of debased coinage in various forms. Whatever were the true forces behind many debasements, they likely included various elements of both coercion and encouragement.

Debasements, like ordinary dilution of primitive monies, directly caused the saleableness of the money to deteriorate. Individuals, when forced to abide by debasement edicts in one way or another, saw their future purchasing power diminish as a consequence. In this way, it is important to understand that should such a hit in terms of salability be large enough, an economy would sooner or later have to revert to a harder primitive money which is, again, only diluted through a painstaking production process. This occurred, for example, in 1st century A.D. China as a response to excessive counterfeiting[25]. Some costs related to the easiness of which many primitive monies were produced had, in other words, partially changed form to instead reveal other costs closely related to power over both money and subjects. Similar to the economic forces affecting many primitive societies, the economic hardships even moderate debasements of metallic coinage could impose on societies may have caused similarly destructive outcomes: debased defense capabilities resulting in bloody conquests by aggressive

---

[24] (Hughes, Crump, & Johnson, 1897, p. 188)
[25] (Einzig, 1949, p. 256)

neighbors. With all that in mind, it is time to proceed in Battúta's footsteps again, this time with a slightly different set of lenses.

11. 'Black' Silver Dirhams of Egypt

As we know by now, Battúta passed through Egypt multiple times during his travels. At the time, that state was the Mamluk Sultanate, or *Dawlat al-Atrāk* ("State of the Turks", which is why Battúta referred to the Mamluk soldiers as Turks when in war-torn 'Aydhab). It must have been interesting for him to arrive to Cairo since more or less all other central points of past Muslim glory were at the time desolate from Mongol invasions, or at the very least besieged by nomad Arabs, Bedouins or by various Christian armies. Cairo, or "al-Qahirah", meaning "the victorious", had been founded by the Fatimids a few centuries earlier, and still held true to its early character. Battúta was evidently impressed:

> *I arrived at length at Cairo, mother of cities*
> *and seat of Pharaoh the tyrant, mistress of broad*
> *regions and fruitful lands, boundless in multitude*
> *of buildings, peerless in beauty and splendor, the*
> *meeting-place of comer and goer, the halting-place*

of feeble and mighty, whose throngs surge as the waves of the sea, and can scarce be contained in her for all her size and capacity. (Battúta, 1325-1354, p. 50)

Despite its foreign and curious name, the Mamluk Sultanate was perhaps also the state entity culturally closest to the Caliphate of previous centuries. The roots of the Mamluks stemmed from the Sunni Muslim Ayyubid dynasty, which in turn had replaced the Fatimid Caliphate. Established by the well-known Kurdish general Saladin in the 12th century, the Ayyubid state (from Saladin's father Ayyub) soon enough included all of Egypt, the Holy Land, the western parts of the Arabian Peninsula, and parts of Syria and Iraq. The Mamluks themselves were slave warriors imported by the Arabs, and they often consisted of Turkic peoples, Circassians, Abkhazians, Albanians, Greeks, and Slavs. By constituting a strong, institutional military cast, the curious installation paved the way for a later overthrow of the Ayyubid masters.

With the sacking of Baghdad by a large force of Mongols under Hulagu Khan, the throne of the Ayyubids was finally up for the taking, and this is exactly what happened after a Mamluk army defeated the Mongols at Ain Jalut in modern day Israel. Despite delivering victory against both Mongols and Crusaders, the Mamluks were alienated and threatened by Ayyubid Sultan Al-Mu'azzam Turan-Shah, up to the point that they rebelled, killed the Sultan in April 1250 A.D., and installed Izz al-Din Aybak as the first Mamluk ruler of Egypt. The slaves had replaced the masters and suddenly wielded immense power.

The Fatimids

As for the monetary systems used in these various dynasties, it should first be mentioned that the tampering of the money had been prevalent even before the ascension of the Mamluks, and in fact even before Ayyubid rule as well. Paul Balog, after researching the many different silver dirhams of Egypt, states that for many consecutive Fatimid rulers whom all preceded Saladin's Ayyubid dynasty, the fine silver content gradually decreased from around 80%, to 66% during the reign of Al-Hakim, to around 50% during the reign of Al-Zahir and Al-Mustansir, and finally to as low as 25% during the reign of Al 'Adid (Balog, 1961, p. 122). It was a "slow but inexorable process of impoverishment". The alloy usually contained copper which darkened the coins to the point that they were called *dirhems waraq*, or "black dirhams".

Balog has a number of examples where under Fatimid rule, silver dirhams lost considerable value against the less traded gold dinars. In 371H (981 A.D.) as well as in 390H (1000 A.D.), a gold dinar was worth 20 silver dirhams, as opposed to 15.5 silver dirhams at the time of Cairo's construction. The stability over the last two decades was likely owed to the red-haired Sultan Al-Aziz, who appears not to have debased his minted silver coins.

In 395 H (1004 A.D.), however, a crisis appears to have started under the reign of Al-Hakim, resulting in the exchange rate dropping over the following years, first to 26, then to 34. Some historical sources indicate that the old dirhams had been cut (*z'aida, qat'a*). In any case, the corrupted dirhams had to be forcibly withdrawn and replaced by new coins at the rate of four old dirhams against one new coin (Balog, 1961, p. 115). It may be considered likely that this exchange rate was worse than how the market priced the different coins. The worst silver dirhams were minted by Al 'Adid however, which is rather fitting as he became the last Arab Sultan of Egypt.

The Ayyubids

Saladin, in other words, had obtained a Sultanate used to enduring the sufferings of debasements. Trying to restore some faith in the money, he withdrew the "black" dirhams and issued so called *Nasiri* dirhams – containing equal parts silver and copper – but since very few have survived until this day, the measure was likely unsuccessful (Balog, 1961, p. 123). What has survived, however, are many new "black" dirhams also from the reign of Saladin, and also with pitiful silver content. The next proposed monetary reform came during the reign of Al-Kamil, where more or less the entire silver currency was to be withdrawn again and replaced by new dirhams supposedly containing two thirds silver, the rest being copper. Balog believes this reform to have been a huge fraud, as the average silver content tested for the new "round" dirhams (as opposed to the "black" dirhams), was around 27%. In other words, Al-Kamil appears to have changed the shape of the money while lowering the silver content to below even that of most "black" dirhams.

It is apparent that more or less all Ayyubid rulers minted highly diluted coins, and this was often reflected in the bad shape of the Egyptian economy. Balog believes the "black" dirhams to have been the bulk of all money used in economic exchange, which must have had repercussions on inflation as copper is more abundant than silver. The people could not easily or affordably assess the silver content in coins, which is likely why the silver money was targeted by the authorities. What about the gold dinars? It appears that around the time of the Fatimid dynasty, the supposedly inexhaustible sources of that precious metal from gold mines in Nubia, or from the numerous ancient tombs, ran out. Egypt had no silver mines either, which meant any import of goods resulted in gold and silver escaping the country.

The Mamluks

As the slave soldiers took over, they seem to initially have kept the silver dirhams relatively pure. In 770H (1369 A.D.), a crisis appears to have occurred and the silver dirham exchange rate fell to 30:1 against the dinar. Further hardship struck the public in

781H (1379 A.D.) as still circulating *Kameli* and *Zaheri* dirhams were altered by the emission of new *Mahmudi* dirhams. This happened under al-Mansur Ali II. Some years later, the new Sultan Barquq issued dirhams that were valued at the rate of 30:1. In 794H (1392 A.D.), Barquq ordered the minting of a large quantity of copper coins called *fulus*. As Egypt had little native copper, it was all imported from Europe and paid for with silver. Barquq's son Faraj eventually inherited the throne, and silver had more or less ceased to partake in Egyptian commerce, which was now conducted in copper *fels* (Balog, 1961, p. 134). The country's money, in other words, had now regressed back to the form it took in Ancient times, and silver became mainly a unit of account.

Faraj tried to fix the copper *fels* exchange rate to the gold dinar at 100:1. But as copper more easily floods any nation adopting it as money, the exchange rate proceeded to fall to 250:1. To counter the bad economic condition of his country, Faraj tried to introduce a gold standard based on that of Venice, but failed. Conditions only improved under Sultan Muayyad Shaik, who minted pure silver dirhams from which "the population rejoiced" (Balog, 1961, p. 135). This relief was short-lived, however, as copper coins continued to be issued, while silver dirhams gradually and continuously disappeared under the Burji Mamluks. Having once stood at a 15.5:1 exchange ratio to the gold dinar, the worthless copper "dirham" of the Mamluks fell as low as 460:1. Further evidence supporting monetary troubles can be seen in the *kiswa* (cloth) allowances given to Mamluk soldiers in the 15th century:

> *Since about the middle of the ninth/fifteenth century there was a steady increase of the kiswa allowance. The allowance rose so steeply as to constitute a real increase despite the deterioration of the dirham (in which coin the allowance was paid) in the corresponding period. In 842/1438*

> *the contemporary historian states that up to that*
> *year the custom was to pay 500 dirhams for the*
> *kiswa. After a hard and protracted struggle the*
> *allowance was raised in the same year to 1000*
> *dirams for a Royal Mamluk, and to 1500 dirhams*
> *for a khassaki. In 855/1451 the sum of 1000*
> *dirhams was considered the normal allowance,*
> *but the mamluks refused to take it until it had*
> *been raised to 2000 dirhams. [...] When the*
> *members of the inferior unit of awlad an-nas*
> *received 2000 dirhams for their kiswa in 918/1512*
> *they were thought to have been gravely wronged*
> *by Ibn Iyas. (Ayalon, 1958, p. 258)*

Since silver dirhams, few as they were, often also were relatively pure under the Mamluks (unlike under the Fatimids and Ayyubids), they had ceased to partake in every-day commerce. It can therefore be hypothesized that the soldiers were paid either in copper "dirhams" (but perhaps with silver still as some vague unit of account) or in some variant of diluted or shrunken silver dirhams. There would otherwise be little reason for resentment with a doubling or even quadrupling of the *kiswa* allowance.

Even the daily Mamluk meat rations were eventually debased in a sense. Defined as a certain weight, amir Manjak al-Yusufi, according to Ayalon, proceeded to give the soldiers unskinned instead of skinned meat. This situation deteriorated towards the end of Mamluk rule:

> *In the last decades of Mamluk rule a new*
> *stereotyped phrase, entirely unknown before,*
> *appears in Mamluk sources with increasing*
> *frequency, viz. "the arrears of the pay for the meat*
> *ration" (al-lahm al-muattal or al-maksur or al-*
> *munkasir). It is true that already in the time of al-*

Maqrizi (died in 845/1442) the Royal Mamluks suffered from time to time from the scarcity of meat and had to eat boiled beans (al-ful al-masluq) instead, and that a similar scarcity existed in 860/1456; yet all these shortages were of a temporary character, whereas the meat shortage of the last 4 decades or so of Mamluk rule was a chronic phenomenon which became increasingly acute. At first the delay in the pay of the meat ration did not exceed 3 months, then it rose to 4, 6, 7 and even 10 months. In the last days of Qansuh al-Ghawri (died 922/1516) the meat debt in the office of the Vizirate reached 40 000 dinars. (Ayalon, 1958, p. 260)

During these times of a scarcity of essentials, Mamluk soldiers regularly raided the Cairo markets. Balog concludes the sad end of the Mamluk reign, occurring one year after the meat shortages mentioned by Ayalon:

The economic confusion and distress continued now until the final collapse of the Mamluk empire in 922H (1517 AD), when the victorious 'Othmanlis put an end to Egypt's independence. (Balog, 1961, p. 145)

12. Money of the 'Franji'

Battúta, while passing the reconquered Holy Land, appears to have been somewhat sympathetic to the hardship of Christian pilgrims whom he observed had to pay considerable fees to reach their holy places. Such extortion rackets were likely a natural result of the long wars with the often hated Franks, or "Franji", that had relatively recently been expelled:

> In the bottom of the same valley is a church venerated by the Christians, who say that it contains the grave of Mary. In the same place there is another church which the Christians venerate and to which they come in pilgrimage. This is the church of which they are falsely persuaded to believe that it contains the grave of Jesus. All who come on pilgrimage to visit it pay a stipulated tax to the Muslims, and suffer very unwillingly various humiliations. [...]

> *Thence I went to Ajalún making in the direction of Ládhiqíya, and passing through the Ghawr, followed the coast to 'Akká [Acre], which is in ruins. Acre was formerly the capital and port of the country of the Franks in Syria, and rivalled Constantinople itself. (Battúta, 1325-1354, pp. 57-58)*

Battúta also appears to have had some preconceived notions of this animosity because he took note when Italian merchants let him on their ship for free, and was greatly surprised by some of the kind reception he got later in Constantinople.

Dauphine Debasements

While the traveler rode through this land and perhaps mused on the dealings and doings of the conquerors and the conquered, it is with not a little amount of irony that the Hundred Years' War was just about to start in North-Western Europe, showing the true colors of Christian Brotherhood. France, one of the main actors in the war, often accrued large revenues from minting activities (63% of total revenue in 1327 A.D.). The situation has been described by Rolnick, Velde and Weber, who paint a rather brusque picture of what was going on up there:

> *In France, the silver currency went through 123 debasements between 1285 and 1490. Of these, 112 reduced the silver content of the currency by more than 5 percent. The single largest debasement reduced it by 50 percent. Gold coinage changed comparatively less in the same period: there were 64 debasements, 48 of which were by more than 5 percent. (Rolnick, Velde, & Weber, 1996, p. 793)*

The 1354-1490 A.D. minting data that these researchers gathered estimates a gross seigniorage rate during "normal" years of 7.5% for silver and 2.0% for gold. In debasement years, however, the number rose to 21.7% and 4.3% respectively. The worst period in France was 1419-1422 A.D., where the rate fluctuated between 40% and 60%. For those years, over 90% of the French Dauphine state revenues could be attributed to seigniorage, and the nominal value of the silver *livre tournois* was set to increase by a factor of 35, far above that of even English coinage under Henry VIII's infamous legacy from a period termed "The Great Debasement". Multiple theories have been put forward as to why the French embraced debasement of their coins to a higher degree than did the English. It is possible that the French crown was unable to secure lending from Italian bankers (something which the English had managed), and as opposed to the English crown, France did not manage to secure silver or gold through other taxation to the same degree (Sussman, 1993, p. 44). Instead of bickering with local assemblies, the Dauphines, seeing the English and Burgundian armies engulf ever larger parts of France, marched desperately to the mints instead. For the year 1422 A.D., the lowest recorded silver content in supposed silver coinage was 2.8%, at the mint in Romans.

It is unclear how often the public could afford to assay all the new issues at local silversmiths, but it is telling that the French did not debase gold to the same degree as they did their silver. Gold was utilized in international trade, with powerful merchants in a much better position to detect debasements early on. A French populace was easier to fool. Traces of this may be seen in the diary of a Parisian merchant, who first attributes the much higher prices in his city to besieging Burgundians, then to besieging Armagnacs, and finally to besieging English – all over a time period where debasements liberally were carried out. Only a couple of years later, in late 1419 A.D., does he mention a "weak currency", and even in 1421 A.D., after the massive debasements, is he uncertain whether to attribute the high prices to war or the money itself. Discussing the new, debased coins he writes:

> [...] they brought trade very low indeed. No one bought or sold anything except for wine and bread, for if a man took 10 francs in cash [coin] with him he would be very heavily burdened, so that people didn't carry money with them. (Sussman, 1993, p. 63)

The uncertainty observed in the merchant's writing is a sad but essential part of what has been termed the *Cantillon effect*, from Irish-French economist Richard Cantillon. This effect is related to the injection point of the new money supply; the entity conducting the seigniorage is the first to receive the new money and can spend it before a change of relative prices has occurred. The French merchant would have had to spend after said change, with resulting loss of purchasing power.

French adulteration of money reached perhaps its twin peaks in the form of the paper money experiments, first in the beginning of the 18th century under the supervision of Scotsman John Law, and then in the form of the Assignats at the end of that same century. Both these ideological and innovative rejections of boring metallic money turned out to be catastrophic failures, resulting in a depressed economy and ultimately the starvation of French families due to a 150-fold increase in prices (Einzig, 1949, p. 306).

The Edwards of England

Money during the Middle Ages was treated slightly better in England, with fewer and lower debasements in general. Edward I, who succeeded his father in 1272 A.D. while in the Holy Land, implemented various penal measures against the clipping of silver coins and proceeded to execute mostly Jews accused of this, despite being practiced by Christians and Jews alike. He

127

then employed a certain William de Turnemire from Marseilles, who appears to have been greatly organized and reformed the English Mint for the better. Turnemire implemented minting techniques that made clipping much harder. In a minting-related document termed the *Red Book*, the following was written in French:

> [...] *Further, that the King cause to be cried throughout his realm that no man change money or ingots or any manner of silver except at the King's Mint, and that no man be so bold as to carry out of the realm the suppressed money.*
> *(Crump & Hughes, 1895, p. 52)*

The public could take their old, clipped or off-shaped coins and exchange for new ones at the Mint. Yet, the fees at the Mint were bad enough for foreign merchants to instead bring pure, privately minted silver coins from Flanders, causing many various silver currencies to circulate in England at the time (Crump & Hughes, 1895, p. 62). Edward I's new silver coins, however, were greatly admired in Europe, and ultimately so popular that he banned the export of them in 1299 A.D.

Edward II appears to have continued his father's relatively sound policies with regards to money. He was restricted by the barons in the form of the Ordinances of 1311 (Hughes, Crump, & Johnson, 1897, p. 185). It is therefore assumed that the English currency was in sound condition in 1314 A.D. Edward III, son of Edward II, observed more and more "black" (diluted) silver coins in his kingdom, and ordered an inefficient ban on the export of silver in 1331 A.D. The Royal Mint, however, backed with peculiar arguments observable in the Rolls of Parliament, continued with debasing coins both in terms of size and silver content:

> [...] *a large alteration in the Mint price will not help us, but a small one may. A merchant with*

> *silver to sell will come to us rather than to France,*
> *if he knows that our Mint price is calculated in*
> *pieces that look like the old pieces and can pass for*
> *them, but are really lighter; he will hope to export*
> *them to France, buy good French coin with them,*
> *bring that to England and so make a profit on the*
> *round trade. (Hughes, Crump, & Johnson, 1897,*
> *p. 188)*

It appears that, while the coinage was debased, it was for the most part not done in secret, nor was it done to defraud Edward III's creditors (by paying back debt with debased money). For the latter part, the King instead preferred to simply deny some of his debts altogether. One theory of what influenced Edward III's debasements, albeit a naïve one, is the fact that England at the time operated under bimetallism. Since at any point in time it can be argued that coins of one of the two metals are overvalued, this leaves the door wide open for embarking on a slight debasement of such coins. After some time, coins of the other metal might be considered overvalued, and the debasements continue in similar fashion.

Edward III obtained many military victories in France during his campaigns there. But his successors would later have to accept that the French crown was beyond English reach. So while the Dauphine debasements greatly exceeded the English counterparts, and while such events caused considerable long-term harm to that economy, there is a case to be made that in the short run, in the middle of burning war, such revenues might have contributed to France's defensive capabilities, resulting in the slow expulsion of the English. There are obviously many other factors at play in such long-lived conflicts, and we will never know the route an alternative history would have taken.

Monetary mismanagement continued in England under Henry VIII, who had the equally bad habit of beheading his ex-wives. Rolnick, Velde and Weber mention these alterations:

From 1542 to 1551, silver or gold was debased ten times, and the pound sterling lost 83% of its silver content. The gross seigniorage rate went from 2 percent to 57 percent. Yet the volume of minting was so large that the single mint at the Tower of London was not enough, and the sovereign had to open six new mints. (Rolnick, Velde, & Weber, 1996, p. 793)

13. Debasements and Propaganda in the Roman Empire

Embarking from the conquered Holy Land, Battúta set out for Anatolia, an area constituting a clear remnant of a vast Roman Empire long vanished:

> At Ládhiqíya we embarked on a large galley belonging to the Genoese, the master of which was called Martalmín, and set out for the country of the Turks known as Bilád ar-Rúm [Anatolia], because it was in ancient times their land. Later on it was conquered by the Muslims, but there are still large number of Christians there under the government of Turkmen Muslims. We were ten nights at sea, and the Christians treated us kindly and took no passage money from us. *(Battúta, 1325-1354, p. 123)*

Bilád ar-Rúm (also known as the Sultanate of Rum) literally meant "the land of the Greeks", owing to the fact that Arabs had used the word for Greek and Roman interchangeably in the past. In other words, this part of Anatolia had once been part of the mighty Roman Empire, of which only a rather diminished Byzantine Empire still remained.

The money of the Roman Empire has been studied in detail by historians and numismatists, and contains many good examples of how rulers disseminated propaganda to the populace and also how that money in the end was altered to benefit the issuers in the short term, while dooming the empire in the long term. Since the Roman state had no press or radio to utilize for communication purposes, it used the mint, whose produce was sure to reach both rich and poor in the empire's distant provinces. Evidence supporting the propaganda purposes of Roman coinage exists in the quality of their craftsmanship, which surpasses many metal coins today. The coins were meant to be looked at. (Grant, 1952, p. 81)

The American Numismatic Society[26] has provided a good timeline of Roman coinage, which we will use to discuss various issues. The Romans of the 4th century B.C. had no coinage of their own. Instead, rough, odd-shaped lumps of copper or bronze known as *Aes Rude* were used as money, meaning they had to be carefully weighted with each transaction (in fact, the word "estimate" likely stems from this *Aes* money). Such money provides a great example of the transition from what we consider primitive money, to more modern coinage. It was likely used in parallel with livestock money (Einzig, 1949, p. 235). Later, rectangular bars of the same alloy, termed *Aes Signatum*, were employed for the same purpose. The first real step towards coinage was arguably *Aes Formatum*, shaped like a bun or a biscuit (Quiggin, 1949, p. 275). It was only after establishing closer contact with the Greek city states on the southernmost part

---

[26] See (American Numismatic Society, 2002)

of the Italian peninsula, that the people of Rome slowly started to appreciate Greek silver coinage as a complement to their own new bronze cast coinage, *Aes Grave*, which they had employed since 289 B.C. Roman silver coins were struck in southern Italy around 280 B.C., and as with much else in Roman society, they imitated the Greek *didrachm* counterparts closely. The cumbersome burden of having to transport copper money across increasingly vast trade networks was thus lessened.

Gods, Heroes and Victories

In 269 B.C. silver coins were minted in the city Rome for the first time, fittingly depicting the twins Romulus and Remus and the she-wolf. It is from that very event that the word "mint" also originated. The famous silver *denarius* was introduced around 217 B.C. and ran successfully and more or less undiluted for centuries. From depicting gods or the deeds of mythical ancestors, the *denarii* started to depict contemporary events around the time of Julius Caesar – one example being an elephant trampling a dragon, which symbolized Caesar's victory over the Gauls. In 44 B.C. a portrait of a living Roman – again Julius Caesar – appeared on the coinage for the first time, setting a new coin standard in the empire. Caesar was also the first to standardize the pure gold *aureus* coins, and he struck them more often than his predecessors. After Caesar's assassination, Brutus, in an attempt to justify the murder, issued a *denarius* depicting a cap of liberty flanked by two daggers. In yet another attempt to solidify personal claims, the grandnephew of Caesar, Octavian, used Caesar's prior deification in his propaganda as he issued coins depicting himself together with the modest statement *DIVI F(ilius)*, or "the son of a god".

Mark Antony soon became embroiled in the politics of Egypt as he initiated an intimate relationship with Cleopatra. The Senate, fearing Mark Antony was compromising Rome's interests, declared war on him and sent Octavian as commander of the legions. After Mark Antony's troops refused to fight for him (likely a result of him paying with debased silver coinage), he committed suicide and Octavian triumphantly issued coins bearing his head and on the reverse a crocodile – symbolizing his victory in Cleopatra's realm. Octavian's son Tiberius utilized his father's supposed divinity in his issuance, just as Octavian once had. Tiberius issued coins depicting the goddess of safety and welfare, Salus, and a reference to Tiberius' own lineage, indicating the empire was safe only under their guidance. Claudius, after completing what Caesar had started with Britain, issued *aureus* coinage with the description *DE BRITANN(is)*. Vespasian, after crushing a Jewish rebellion that began under Nero, minted coins where he stood as an emperor in military gear, and with a foot on a helmet. Nearby a Jewess was seated under a palm tree, representing submission. The coin description read *IVDAEA CAPTA*, which should need no explanation.

The rule of Vespasian from 69 A.D. – a result of the civil war originating from emperor Nero's suicide – might be said to have helped advance something ominous that Nero himself initiated after a fire had consumed Rome: the peace-time debasement of Roman coinage. The *denarius* under Vespasian's reign saw its silver content reduced from 93.5% to 90%. Necessities of war had sometimes compelled emperors and generals to debase the coinage that was used to pay the legions, but in times of peace, the Roman Empire had so far been greatly spared from such ill-fated practices.

A 'Kingdom of Rust'

Rome's expansion under the Republic had brought silver and gold booty, as well as fruitful mines, into its arms. As soon as those sources got ever more depleted, however, a problem arose in how to pay the legions. Rather than trying to increase direct taxation or cut other costs, the state obtained more and more of its funds from the adulteration of its coinage. Kevin Butcher, in his *Debasement and the decline of Rome*, attributes much of the empire's decline to such debasements.

While debasements now became a regularly used tool for Roman emperors, propaganda continued unabashed as well. Hadrian, wanting to emphasize a benevolent attitude towards the various provinces, issued gold coins around 135 A.D., of him extending a hand to a kneeling province, Achaea (Greece). A depicted amphora helped the coin owner recognize the province.

The Roman Empire continued its stride on a wrong path as Commodus took over the sole reign after his father Marcus Aurelius died. Contemporary historian Cassius Dio perfectly captured the essence of this decline in his writings:

> *This matter [of Commodus] must be our next topic; for our history now descends from a kingdom of gold to one of iron and rust, as affairs did for the Romans of that day. (Cassius, A.D. 164–229, p. 69)*

Not only did Commodus debase the coinage further, but he also developed megalomania that manifested itself in boastful statues portraying a giant, and a demi-god. As Rome was struck by a fire in 191 A.D., Commodus saw an opportunity and modestly declared himself the new Romulus after the fire had been extinguished. He also changed the names of the twelve months of the year to correspond to his own twelve names.

A notable reduction of the *denarius* silver content occurred under Septimius Severus in the early 3rd century. Inheriting a silver *denarius* of 81.5% purity, Septimius Severus brought the purity down to first 78.5%, then to 64.5%, followed by 54% – all due to military expenses. Accumulated, his debasements became the largest since Nero. The *antoninianus*, worth two *denarii*, was introduced by Caracella in early 215 A.D. Initially, the content of the new coinage consisted of 75% pure silver, but this double denomination would soon suffer further debasements like its *denarii* counterparts. Since the older *denarius* often contained a higher silver purity despite the dilution, such coins were hoarded, while the *antoninianus* would be spent first. During the second half of the 3rd century, the silver content of the *antoninianus* fell to just 2%. More evidence of large-scale money production is found in the number of mint workers involved in a revolt in Rome under Aurelian, in a battle that left thousands dead (Butcher, 2015, p. 194).

Gallienus, around 258 A.D., tried to improve morale of his troops by issuing coins depicting the various legions. The worthless, token-like coinage, compared by a 19th century German historian to "papiergeld", and referred to in the French translation as *"l'assignat"* (Butcher, 2015, p. 189) was discontinued as the very same troops abandoned Gallienus for a usurper. This debasement further caused a financial crisis, resulting in banks refusing to accept the new coins altogether. In 268 A.D the empire had split into three different states, but was later restored under Aurelian and Diocletian. But the century proved very difficult for the Romans. Gold was rare and most silver coins had been debased to oblivion.

A surprising but futile effort of strengthening the imperial coinage was undertaken by Aurelian in 274 A.D. He increased the silver content of silver coins to just under 5%. The silver content in the coinage continued to decrease later on, however, which caused the authorities under Diocletian to enact laws that limited prices on goods and services. Any economist worth his *sal* would have told the emperor that such attempts are counterproductive and that they almost always are ignoring the cause of the price increases: monetary inflation. Sellers and producers, not being able to make a profit anymore, would stop providing the market with goods, or sell them illegally. The Roman price control edict of 301 A.D. failed, despite Diocletian threatening both buyer and seller with death.

In a last attempt to salvage the failing monetary system of the empire, Diocletian issued the *argentus* silver coin with the same purity as that of a Roman *denarius* before Nero's debasements. It was too late, however, and Rome soon enough fell into a state of civil wars and chaos – a result of Diocletian's extensive taxation measures, the tampering with the coinage, price laws, and brutal religious persecution. Ludwig von Mises attributes the fall of Rome to such economic mismanagement as well (Mises, 1949, pp. 761-763). It is arguable that the fine silver coinage briefly initiated by Diocletian carried over to Constantine the Great, who broke from his predecessors' monetary illiteracy by issuing large quantities of pure gold *solidus* coins in his new Eastern Roman Empire. As the West fell, the East lasted for another thousand years, and as we soon shall see, it was the mismanagement of money that helped cripple also that empire in the end.

14. Coinage and the 'Lydian Disease'

No book on ancient monetary systems is complete without also some words on the Lydians, whose empire now is long gone. Unnoticeable signs of it perhaps manifested themselves to Battúta and his company when the journey took them to southwestern Anatolia, where Greeks had been living for more than two thousand years. One of these sites was Ephesus, which had just recently been conquered by the Turks:

> We went on through the town of Tíra, which is in the territories of this sultan, to Ayá Sulúq [Ephesus], a large and ancient town venerated by the Greeks. It possesses a large church built of finely hewn stones each measuring ten or more cubits in length. The central cathedral mosque, which was formerly a church greatly venerated by the Greeks, is one of the most beautiful in the world. (Battúta, 1325-1354, p. 134)

The Birth of 'Eastern Decadence'

Ephesus was on the exact intersection between Greek and Lydian culture, and was therefore one of the places where the Greek settlers could observe their Anatolian neighbors; the Lydian capital of Sardis was situated only a short travel to the east. To this closeness is owed the mixed skepticism and awe many Greeks felt for Lydians in general, which Herodotus sums up in his writing:

> *All the young women of Lydia sell themselves, by which they procure their marriage-portion; this they afterwards dispose of as they think proper. [...]. The manners and customs of the Lydians do not essentially vary from those of Greece, except in this sale of the young women. They are the first people on record who coined gold and silver into money, and traded in retail. They claim also the invention of certain games, which have since been practiced among the Grecians [...]. (Herodotus, 440 B.C., p. 79)*

As Herodotus mentions, Greek settlers adopted much from the Lydians, both with regards to culture and religion. They were likely impressed also by the coinage, just as the Romans later were impressed by the Greek coinage they stumbled upon in the southern parts of Italy. Yet, due to some sharp distinctions of the cultures, Greeks also brought back a notion of "Eastern decadence", or the "Lydian decease", or "Lydian-living" – a view which ironically the Romans later reserved for the Greeks themselves. Alexandra Gruca-Macaulay explored this stereotype:

> *Athenaeus explains the "the Lydians were notorious for luxorious living; in fact the word 'Lydian-living' in Anacreon is understood to*

139

> *mean the same as 'luxurious living'". The*
> *association between Lydians and decadent*
> *luxuria was well-established in ancient times and*
> *has been attested in both literature and art.*
> *(Gruca-Macaulay, 2016, p. 127)*

How variants of this expression was adopted by the Romans can for example be observed in some Roman poems, where the author opposes the decision of his friend to leave for "mollis Ionia", meaning soft, decadent Ionia (Gold, 2012). Perhaps something else advancing this view was the Greeks trying to make sense of the quick fall of Lydia to the Persians under Cyrus the Great.

An Immaculate Conception?

As for the minting of coins, it appears to have started no later than 600 B.C., in western Anatolia. Researchers do not fully agree whether it was the Lydians or the Greeks, or even wealthy private merchants that initiated this standardization of electrum (a natural alloy of white gold) bullion into actual coinage, but what they do seem to agree on is the main aim being better commerce through increased fungibility. It was not random that the Lydians or Greeks first introduced coinage; Herodotus called Lydians "the first shopkeepers", and trade had long flourished in the area due to superior natural harbors, Eastern caravans, and a high number of native goods demanded by foreigners (Quiggin, 1949, p. 282). Fitting in our saleableness framework, standardization lowered the cost of transacting in precious metals as the coins could start circulating by tale and not by weight. Yet, while the electrum coinage in question became more uniform in terms of size and weight, it was still hard to make uniform its actual content. Robert W. Wallace mentions a silver content of the natural electrum between 10-30% (Wallace, 1987, p. 386). King Croesus of Lydia minted electrum coins with 27%

silver according to Herodotus, yet most early electrum coins had a silver content closer to 50%, indicating many had been rather heavily debased. And it is with this last observation that our understanding of this earliest coinage ought to take a cynical turn. If it was fungibility the issuer was after, why debase the electrum coinage, and why not strike silver- and gold coins as well?

Wallace commented on the curious discrepancy that only electrum was made into coinage: "The restriction of electrum alloy is an important and idiosyncratic feature of the earliest coinage, a feature that needs to be explained." (Wallace, 1987, p. 388). Some of the speculations regarding why coins were minted in electrum in the first place, and not from gold- or silver bullion, are indeed rather cynical. Yet, they are also in line with what we have so often observed with regards to metallic money – the allure of seigniorage. By striking coins in electrum and not pure silver or gold, could the public be defrauded somehow? Lydians and Greeks did have access to silver, as is indicated by the electrum coin debasements, and Anatolia even contained silver mines at the time. Gold was readily available as well, supported by evidence from Sardis. It is, however, not fully established whether the method of cementation[27] was known in Lydia at the time, and some evidence points to the fact that it wasn't. This meant that the owner of electrum bullion likely had no way to create pure silver- and gold bullion from that alloy, and so instead had to figure out how to increase fungibility in other ways.

An argument concerning fraud was first put forward by Bolin, who called the whole introduction of Lydian coinage "an imposture, a large-scale swindle" (Wallace, 1987, p. 387), pointing to the fact that the coinage was artificially debased. Bolin, however, did not know at the time that the silver content

---

[27] Cementation meant the silver and gold could be fully separated from electrum.

of electrum in nature varied, which may explain his deep skepticism when assessing such coinage with above average silver content. Yet, even if he had known that fact, the higher-than-average silver content would have had to be explained somehow. But there are acceptable theories to that as well; the high gold content naturally occurring in Lydian electrum caused the coinage to be inconveniently valued. Only by diluting it with silver before striking coins could even the smallest denomination function as everyday medium of exchange.

Related to the natural content variation of electrum is another theory of why the Lydians and Greeks first made coins only from such bullion; if the gold content of electrum varied greatly, merchants would not readily accept such money without weighing and assessing carefully. By putting an official stamp on the electrum (causing it to become coinage), it is possible that the issuer wanted to lessen this uncertainty without a costly or even, at the time, unknown cementation process, either by indicating some form of redeemability to other types of commodities, or perhaps more realistically by signaling that coins of the same issue at least could be trusted to contain the same gold- and silver content. To what degree such considerations played a role, we cannot be certain. One explanation that should not quickly be discarded, however, is as we know, seigniorage, attested by the fact that assessing the gold content of electrum coinage or bullion was difficult. By striking electrum and silver bullion into coins, stamped with marks of quality, such coins could temporarily function as a convenient medium of exchange while perhaps enriching the issuers by obfuscating the actual gold content. If cementation was indeed unknown at the time, it may even have been the case that electrum was sold as a valuable precious metal on its own, making dilution a profitable business. Archimedes had not been born yet, and so the Lydians and the Greeks had no way of being 100% certain that the shining, white metal found by local river beds, indeed consisted of two other precious metals.

It wouldn't take long before electrum fell out of fashion again (likely as cementation became known and widespread), and the civilized world, including Lydia, adopted pure gold- and silver money instead due to the superior saleableness of such bullion and coinage.

15. 'Bad Money' of the Byzantine Empire

The sick, wounded man that was Rome, which we have spoken about, settled in Constantinople under Constantine the Great and was soon to thrive again under better money. But the centuries passed and the pure gold coinage of Constantine became an ever more ancient relic. And so it was after having escorted a Greek princess married to Öz Beg Khan, to the Byzantine Empire's capital, that Battúta first mentioned the decadent state of the money used there:

> When it became clear to the Turks who were in the khátún's [the princess's] company that she professed her father's religion [Christianity] and wished to stay with him, they asked her for leave to return to their country. She made them rich presents and sent them an amir called Sarúja with five hundred horsemen to escort them to their

> *country. She sent for me, and gave me three*
> *hundred of their gold dinars, called barbara,*
> *which are not good money, and a thousand*
> *Venetian silver pieces, together with some robes*
> *and pieces of cloth and two horses, which were a*
> *gift from her father, and commended me to Sarúja.*
> (Battúta, 1325-1354, p. 164)

Öz Beg Khan's third wife, in other words, had only nominally embraced Islam. Battúta mentions her drinking wine and eating swine, which likely caused some anguish for him and his company as they now faced a large force of Greek soldiers welcoming their princess. But although not truly a Muslim, the princess still showed an interest in Battúta and his friends' wellbeing, as she was quick to punish a Greek cavalryman laughing at the Muslims as they prayed on the ground.

The *barbara* of which Battúta spoke was, according to H.A.R Gibb, the debased *hyperpyron*. The story of Byzantine money is, as was the case with much contemporary coinage, slightly different from that of primitive monies since it was Greek Emperors and not foreign traders that debased it. Certain aspects of the dynamics of money remained the same however, as we soon shall see.

First Signs of Decay

Although the history of the Empire goes far back, we will enter it with the ascension of Leo III (Leo the Isaurian) in the year 716 A.D., as his extensive reforms are what caused many historians to separate the Eastern Roman Empire from the Byzantine Empire. The Empire had, prior to the sound reforms, been in a rather drastic decline, with taxes extracted from the populace to such a degree that not enough savings could arrest a decline in the amount of capital. In other words, factories, farms and infrastructure fell into disrepair. Aggressive neighbors had conquered many provinces. But Leo did in fact inherit a monetary system of undiluted gold coins known as *bezants* in Europe; these were the *solidus* coins that Constantine prudently had introduced centuries earlier. And there was still some life in the old Roman legal system that favored and facilitated commerce, so Leo the Foreigner, against all odds, managed to save the Empire from imploding.

Leo was not the only Byzantine regent struggling with an empty treasury in the face of famines, wars, natural disasters and varying degrees of a malfunctioning administration, and to his credit, he, unlike many others, did not touch the Empire's money. Some of the first mentions of such practices relates to the reign of Nikephoros II Phokas. Crowned in the end of the 10th century, he adopted policies aimed at strengthening the Byzantine military that had become wholly reliant on foreign mercenaries. For these policies he needed money, and despite curtailing expenses related to courtier pensions and monasteries, those were not enough. George Finley, in his monumental *History of the Byzantine Empire*, mentions Nikephoros' strategy that sowed the seed to Battúta's disappointment:

> *The worst act of his [Nikephoros II] reign, and one for which the Byzantine historians have justly branded him with merited odium, was his violation of the public faith, and the honour of the Eastern Empire, by adulterating the coin, and issuing a debased coin, called the tetarteron. This debased money he employed to pay the debts of the state, while the taxes continued to be extracted in the old and pure coin of the empire. The standard of the coinage of the Eastern Empire, it must always be borne in mind, remained always the same until the taking of Constantinople by the Crusaders. The gold coins of Leo III. [8th century] and of Isaac II. [12th-13th century] are of the same*

weight and purity; and the few emperors who disgraced their reigns by tampering with the currency have been branded with infamy. (Finlay, History of the Byzantine and Greek empires, from DCCXVI to MLVII., 1853, p. 389)

Nikephoros II's unpopularity had him murdered on the 10th December 969 A.D., by ambitious relatives in his own palace. Although Nikephoros II by no means was a decadent despot in other regards (usually living as a soldier, he preferred to sleep on the floor and not in his royal bed), his main legacy seems to have been the act of debasing the empire's pure money. Nikephoros II's reign was succeeded by various emperors – some good and some bad. Periodically, taxation was increased to the degree that it caused much suffering. One anecdote from Michael IV's reign describes the emperor and his sister traveling to Ephesus and consequently having to witness the misery of the poorer part of the population outside of the capital. Michael's sister implored him to lower their tax burden, whereupon he coldly answered "You reason like a woman, ignorant of the necessities of the imperial treasury".

The newborn tradition of debasing the empire's coinage continued under the reign of Constantine IX Monomachus, likely due to a costly war against a massive army of Pechenegs, and has been detailed by Costas Kaplinis in his article *The Debasement of the "Dollar of the Middle Ages"*. It appears that little is documented regarding Constantine IX's acts of debasement, but uncovered numismatic evidence revealed a drop in gold content of the *bezants* of around 10 percentage points. A lighter coin, the *tetarteron*, was debased by around 20% (Kaplanis, 2003, p. 770). George Finley marked the reign of Constantine IX as the start of a slow, inevitable decline.

A Debased Defense

The instability of the Empire led to revolts, usurpers, and general unrest. After a Byzantine loss in the battle of Manzikert against Seljuk Turks in 1071 A.D., the reigns of emperors were often short lived. At the time of Romanus IV, who was captured at Manzikert, the gold content of *bezants* seems to have been around 70%. Nikephorus III, an incompetent man more interested in royal parties than in administrating his empire, wasted vast sums of public money and debased the coinage[28]. Not long after his short reign ended, Constantinople was sacked by Slavs, Bulgarians and Greeks in revolt, marking yet another clear point in the decline of the Empire.

The reign of Alexius I, coronated in 1081 A.D., fared little better:

> *The unpopularity of Alexius among the people was caused by the severity with which the public taxes were collected, by the injustice of the monopolies he created for the profit of the fisc and of members of the imperial family, and by the frauds he committed in adulterating the coinage. This mode of cheating his subjects was carried to a greater extent by Alexius than it had been by any of his predecessors, and it is the strongest symptoms of the incurable decline in the government of the Byzantine empire. [...] Alexius paid the public debts in his own debased coinage, but he enforced payment of the taxes, as long as it was possible, in the pure coinage of earlier emperors. (Finlay, History of the Byzantine and*

---

[28] (Finlay, History of the Byzantine and Greek empires, from MLVII to MCCCCLIII., 1854, p. 57)

Greek empires, from MLVII to MCCCCLIII.,
1854, pp. 75-76)

When later dealing with the other nations in Europe (where pure Byzantine gold coinage had circulated freely and with huge success), Alexius was humiliatingly forced to stipulate that he was paying with coins carrying the portrait of other emperors than himself. In addition to causing a loss of faith in public dealings with the empire, Byzantine commerce in the Mediterranean declined as well. The credit of Greek merchants was soon ruined and large amounts of capital transferred to the republics of Italy. The gold content of the *bezants* under Alexius had fallen to as low as 10% before the introduction of a new gold coin called the *hyperpyron* (which, as we know, Battúta later observed debased and bastardized). Yet, the Empire suffered many long decades with Alexius before he died and was succeeded by his son John II (Comnenus), who was much more capable.

Administrative mismanagement continued up to the point that a force of Latins (mainly Italians), temporarily managed to break the Byzantine Empire. George Finley summed up that event:

> *A despotism supported by personal influence soon ruined the scientific fabric which had previously upheld the imperial power. The people were ground to the earth by a fiscal rapacity, over which the splendor of the house of Comnenus throws a thin veil. The wealth of the empire was dissipated, its prosperity destroyed, the administration of justice corrupted, and the central authority lost all control over the population, when a band of 20,000 adventurers, masked as crusaders, put an end to the Roman empire of the East. (Finlay, History of the*

149

John III, now ruling over the Empire of Nicaea, had multiple good traits, but he continued his predecessors' habit of issuing debased coinage, with only two thirds of it being pure gold. John's son Theodore II carried on with the same coinage composition, while Michael VIII later coined money with only fifteen out of twenty-four parts being pure gold. This last act was cleverly done under the pretense of the need to change the gold coinage to commemorate the recovery of Constantinople from the Latins.

Andronicus II issued coins with fourteen parts gold and ten alloy, and in the end debased it further to equal parts gold and alloy. It is likely that it was the *bezants* of Andronicus II, whose reign lasted until 1328 A.D., that Ibn Battúta observed in Constantinople only a few years later. As a passing and perhaps unimportant testimony to the non-productive, bureaucratic state of the Byzantine Empire at this time, Battúta noted:

> *Most of the population of the city [Constantinople] are monks, ascetics, and priests, and its churches are not to be counted for multitude. (Battúta, 1325-1354, p. 162)*

It should now be clear in what direction the money of the Byzantine Empire, as with that of many other empires now vanquished, was heading. By mixing alloy with the pure gold, emperors could easily cut production costs of money, obtaining immediate seigniorage. So while gold in and of itself can be considered hard money in the sense that it has a high degree of hardness (it was hard to produce more in relation to existing stock), the monopoly of money production by the state made a similar dilution possible anyway. While its *bezant* predecessors had changed hands as far away as India and the British Isles, the newer Byzantine coinage of course fell out of favor as debasements caused it to be despised everywhere.

In 1453 A.D., Emperor Constantine XI's body lay slain among the corpses of his compatriots. The Turks had conquered Constantinople, and many Greek families suddenly found themselves destined for hopeless slavery. It is not possible to estimate to what degree a continuous debasement of the money influenced the Empire's capacity to uphold its borders, but it is highly likely the loss of faith in the monetary system had negative long-term repercussions on commerce, investments and ultimately defense. It is worth adding that after the annihilation of the Byzantine Empire was a fact, and after the brutal dethronement of its last emperor was but a distant memory, pure gold *bezants* continued to be used in commerce for centuries.

16. A Specter over the Eastern Mint

As Ibn Battúta continued his journey through Anatolia, he noticed that the Turks recently had been busy occupying Greek cities and towns there. Him reciting these events counts as one of the first ever written account on the early Ottoman Empire:

> *The sultan of Bursá is Orkhán Bek, son of 'Othmán Chúk. He is the greatest of the Turkmen kings and the richest in wealth, lands and military forces, and possesses nearly a hundred fortresses which he is continually visiting for inspection and putting to rights. (Battúta, 1325-1354, p. 136)*

Wars and Currency Flows

The Ottomans, like their Greek and Roman predecessors, debased their coinage. And as with many of these events, it all seems to have had a connection to costly conflicts – this time against the Safavids in Persia (1532-1555 A.D.). One of the many victims of the war was the pure Ottoman silver *akçe*, which saw a drastic debasement around 1585 A.D. Some economists and historians attributed the act of debasement to the influx of Spanish silver from the Americas to the Ottoman Empire, but fail to provide a comprehensive explanation why that would cause the Ottoman authorities to devalue the silver even further. More abundant silver, being a natural type of debasement by itself, ought if anything, to have called for a centralized reinforcement of the *akçe*, meaning an increase in silver content or weight. So why then did the Ottomans debase their money?

Baki Tezcan, in his research article *The Ottoman Monetary Crisis of 1585 Revisited*, explored this very question and also found the rather lazy nod to American silver unconvincing. And to make matters even more complicated, he found that the Ottoman central treasury, in the midst of the Safavid wars and just before the debasement, was in a rather solid shape (although this is refuted by other sources). The explanation of the debasement, according to him, lay mainly in the empire's various currency zones.

The conquest of Mamluk as well as Safavid provinces had led to the various geographical areas, although loosely governed from Istanbul, to be operating on different types of currencies. Silver coins in former Mamluk lands appear to have been heavier than the *akçe* (Tezcan, 2009, p. 466). But even when accounting for weight differences, it became apparent that silver was highly overvalued in Cairo with a gold-silver ratio around 7:1, while in Istanbul that number was closer to 11:1. This observation is somewhat supported by the documented scarcity of silver in Egypt during the last days of the Mamluks. With the ever closer economic integration of the new provinces, the difference in gold-silver ratios diminished steadily as merchants transported silver from the Ottoman Balkans and Anatolia where it was relatively cheap, to the eastern and southern provinces where it was relatively expensive. (Tezcan, 2009, p. 470). This was something the Ottoman authorities wanted to reverse.

The reason for the unfavorable view of this equalization of gold-silver ratios through the constant east- and southward flow of silver could be found in how taxes were collected. Before the economic integration, taxes from the Arab provinces had consisted mostly of gold which the inhabitants there, as we have established, valued relatively low against silver. As merchants now brought silver coins from all over the empire and beyond to where it was locally overvalued, the downward pressure on the price of silver in the east and south ultimately caused those provinces to pay taxes in silver instead. The arbitrage opportunities of the Ottoman State, in other words, diminished.

It appears, also, that the silver in the empire slowly was drained towards some unknown destination where it was even higher valued than in Egypt, and to counter this, Tezcan argues, both the *akçe* as well as the Ottoman silver coins of Aleppo and Cairo had to be debased. The unknown area in question is thought to have been the empire's Persian holdings, operating mostly under Ottoman silver *sahi* and Persian silver *shahi*. Unlike the *akçe*, the Persian *shahi* had already been debased by 50% in the first half of the 16th century, which might have influenced the silver flows (Tezcan, 2009, p. 474). A more clear-cut explanation of the eastern drain of silver lies in the fact that Ottoman merchants ran a lucrative silk import from Persia, which they funded with silver. All in all, it can be assumed that the plans for the first Ottoman debasement were made partly to counter various silver flows, and also under the guise of a general scarcity of silver at the mints, as has so often been the pretext of these things.

The Debasement of 1585-1586

Combined with the costly war against the Persians as well as against Christian forces in the west, the situation in 1585 A.D.

was finally ripe for a devaluation of Ottoman silver money. Sultan Murad III, who after coming to power had his five younger brothers strangled, had let the war in the east drag on for many years. This helps explain why he deemed it necessary to decrease the silver content of the *akçe* from 0.68 grams to 0.38 grams, causing a doubling of consumer prices over the following three years (Pamuk, 2001, p. 78). Notably, the state did not debase the pure Dutch and Spanish silver coins circulating within its borders, perhaps because as those were used much in foreign trade, a debasement would be noticed and condemned. As for the debasements of the smaller *akçe* coins, it was mainly the poorer part of the Turkish population that was about to be swindled in the heist. That the public, rather unused to the phenomenon, still understood that debasements occurred is supported by Haim Gerber's research:

> But the government could only gain from the debasement if it could somehow make the public go on behaving in the same way as it had before the debasement. Unfortunately, the public thought, no less than the government, that the value of the coin was the value of the precious metal it contained, and refused to be "cheated". This is reflected in the eventual effect of debasement on prices. That prices were fast in following debasements is nicely shown by one Hebrew response from Salonika in which we come across the sentence: "shops became very much more expensive because the money was debased…". (Gerber, 1982, pp. 313-314)

Gerber puts the nominal inflation between 1587 and 1607, in terms of *akçe* and caused by the monetary policy, at 6.4% per year. The annual net inflow of silver to the Ottoman Empire was at a much lower rate.

The standing army of janissaries, having grown considerably at the expense of the older and cheaper feudal army, started to be paid in the debased *akçe,* causing discontent which culminated in the imperial cavalry rebelling and demanding the execution of the vizier Mehmed Pasha. The *timar* (military land grant system) had relied on taxes paid by peasants to the *sipahi* (cavalrymen). These taxes were fixed in terms of the *akçe.* As the cost of living, weapons and armor increased with *akçe* debasements, many *sipahis* ultimately refused to join the army and began to leave their *timars* altogether (Pamuk, 2001, p. 84). Once again a clear link between military capability and monetary policy emerges.

Since the central authorities were slow to adjust their various payment contracts, discontent and instability became the norm, and set in motion a destructive spiral where, as a shortsighted answer to financial difficulties, further debasements were undertaken. The *akçe* would gradually continue to defraud the people as it lost its whole silver content over the next centuries. In the beginning of the 19th century, it had been debased 94% to just 0.048 grams of silver, since its pure conception (Malanima, 2009, p. 198). From the documented disturbances caused to the military, it is likely that this monetary policy helped initiate or at least speed up the decline of the Ottoman Empire. We will end this chapter with a passing remark by the famous French 17th century traveler Jean Chardin, exactly 100 years after the first Ottoman debasement:

> *There are no People in the World that have been more frequently cheated [by bad money], or that are more eafily gull'd then the Turks […].* *(Chardin, 1686, p. 9)*

17. Safavid Poetry

As part of Battúta's second journey – on which he, as we now know, visited the Holy Land and Syria – was a slight detour through the western parts of Persia. Then the Ilkhanate, signs of that Mongol empire's disintegration were palpable:

> *The next day our way lay through orchards and streams and fine villages, with very many pigeon towers, and in the afternoon we reached Isfahán or Ispahán, in 'Iráq al-'Ajam. Isfahán is one of the largest and fairest of cities, but the greater part of it is now in ruins, as a result of the feud between Sunnis and Shi'ites, which is still raging there. (Battúta, 1325-1354, p. 91)*

Debasements under Shāh Tahmāsp

The Ilkhanate was one of the many state entities formed long after the death of Genghis Khan. It would take another three decades for it to fall entirely, only to later be replaced by the

Turco-Mongol Timurid Empire founded by Timur. The power of the Timurids rapidly declined in the second half of the 15th century, and province after province fell from within to the very same Shiite Safavid dynasty that the Ottomans soon thereafter invaded. The Ottoman silver currency debasement of 1585 A.D. had, as we know, been preceded by one such conflict, and it is from an Italian physician traveling in the region that evidence emerged of a contemporary Safavid adulteration of their *shahi* coins as well:

> *Touching the reuenues of this kingdome [Safavid Persia], the common opinion is, that in the dayes of Kinge Tamas [Tahmasp (1524-76)] the crowne did yearely receaue into the Chamber of Casbin, foure or fiue millions of gold, which afterward he caused to be worth eight millions, by a sudden enhaunsing of the value of his coyne, geuing in commandment by most seuere Edictes, that ouer all his Empyre, for a certayne space, all the money that he had receaued, should bee taken and accompted for asmuch more as it was worth, and accordingly made pay to his souldiers and Sultans, & all other that were in his pay. (Tezcan, 2009, p. 474)*

Such a harsh debasement, not only by the fact that the silver content halved, but since the legal enforcement of the value of the debased coins was "severe", actually made it somewhat of an exception. Most acts of debasement in history were gradual so that assessing the silver content with the naked eye, and perhaps even by other means, became impossible or too costly. But if a ruler were to confiscate great sums of money from his subjects, brute force likely became a necessity. The *shahi* debaser in question was none other than Shāh Tahmāsp, and he had already debased the silver content earlier, from 7.88 g. to 6.22 g, then to

5.25 g., and lastly to 4.67 g (Tezcan, 2009, p. 473). The debasement of which the Italian physician speaks, occurred in the end of Tahmāsp's reign, and reduced the silver content to around 2.3 g.

Despite, or perhaps even because of, the above confiscatory monetary policies, Tahmāsp managed to hold off both Ottomans and Uzbeks and stabilize his young empire. Initially pressed from all sides, the situation had in some ways been similar to that of the Dauphines in France during the Hundred Years' War, where they took to short-term beneficial, but long-term harmful, debasements to fund the troops. After campaigns in the Caucasus, Tahmāsp also brought thousands of Christian slaves to the middle of his empire in order to establish *Ghulam* slave corps without the complicated and treacherous tribal affiliations the Shah was used to deal with. In other words, his aim was to model the new military class after the Ottoman janissaries, or the Egyptian Mamluks. But instead of strengthening the empire, it arguably infused further tribalism that would flare up later on.

The Long Fall

Multiple historians have pinpointed the beginning of the end of Safavid Persia to 1629 A.D., when Shah `Abbas I finally died without successors (he had killed or blinded his sons). The blame has often been put on a multitude of non-economic factors: the disappearance of a theocratic nucleus around which the first Shah Ismail had rallied support, ethnic divisions between groups in the military cast, harem shadow governments and the effect a harem upbringing had on future rulers. Laurence Lockhart's massive study on the subject was one of the earliest, and nodding towards orientalism, he put heavy emphasis on the decadent state of the Safavid court. Only a minority of historians have focused on the economy.

John Foran, in his *The Long Fall of the Safavid Dynasty: Moving beyond the Standard Views*, is one of those focusing on, among other things, inflationary dynamics. After first describing the flows of specie through Iran in the silk- and spice trade with India and Europe, Foran arrives at additional causes that always seem to promise economic hardship in the end:

> But in 1677, Chardin remarked, "The money itself has been altered. One no longer encounters good coins." By 1684, most of the coins in circulation were seriously debased; the bazaars at Isfahan were closed, and new money was ordered minted. (Foran, 1992, p. 284)

Upon leaving Persia in 1677, Chardin also reflected upon what he observed was a greatly diminished wealth in the land, compared to his first visit 12 years prior. He, according to Foran, estimated that the Sultan's Harem took up over 10% of the state's expenses. As the expenses for the army also rose, the Shahs resorted to the sale of offices which just exacerbated the crisis. Under Sultan Husayn, the roads, now filled with impoverished peasants taking to banditry, were no longer safe to travel. John Foran concludes:

> My contention is that the result of these various developments was economic deterioration at all levels of society. The drain of currency and debasement of the coins in circulation hurt the merchant classes (and the ulama who depended on their contributions). Military and harem expenditures led to fiscal crisis at the apex of the state, and undermined the Safavid family and the vast number of courtiers and others it supported. In turn this unleashed new abuses such as the sale of offices, corruption, and higher taxes. (Foran, 1992, p. 288)

Rudi Matthee, in his work *Persia in Crisis: Safavid Decline and the Fall of Isfahan*, mentions the 17th century debasements as well. In

1645 A.D., the new `abbasi silver coin was valued at 2 *mahmudis*, as opposed to 2.5 before. It is also during this time period that Sa'ib of Tabriz, court poet under Shah `Abbas II, wrote the following poem:

> *Sa'ib, get yourself some iron object looking*
> *like a coin*
> *because it's merchandise today that's close to*
> *gold*
> *(Matthee, 2011, p. 90)*

Despite a ban on the export of silver (due to what was perceived a scarcity of money), the old and purer `abbasi disappeared from the country in a good example of Gresham's Law. In 1662 A.D., Shah `Abbas II debased the `abbasi with 20%, prompting more poetry on the subject. Merchants quickly turned to foreign gold *ducats* whenever they could, while the poorer population had to endure the debased silver. Some of these merchants, operating under the VOC (Dutch East India Company), melted `abbasis in 1682 A.D. and found the silver content much worse than expected. The continuous debasements resulted in numerous merchant bankruptcies (Matthee, 2011, p. 99).

Finally, Matthee found another telling Persian poem from the 17th century, also revealing the state of the money there:

> *Unrest rose from a deep sleep. People were*
> *weighed down with dirhams, like the fish*
>
> *Isfahan's money is so unworthy, as if there*
> *were a dragon in each money bag*
>
> *The beggar doesn't take money, which is so*
> *abundant that one would say its lion is a man-*
> *eater*

*The world has become so topsy-turvy because
of copper that the fish has become bent under the
earth*

*Gold does not turn white by people's touch.
Everyone who sees it claps his hands from afar*

*The dirham has become so despised by people
that even the rich person has become generous*

*The money's face is like a lion these days old
and young flee for fear of it*

*The creditor flees from the borrower never did
the world see such ways*

*One wishes that the lord of the world in his
bounty would make the dirham a lion catcher*

*Let him make two of those unworthy coins one
so that they become of unquestioned currency*

*The hand of counterfeiters would be cut by the
sword of justice from limb to limb*

*At the time of this upheaval of the dirham I
was worried about abundance and scarcity*

*Reason said: tell me the truth, quickly
When the dirham doubled, gold showed its true
value*

(Matthee, 2011, pp. 91-92)

In 1722 A.D., an Afghan army defeated the Safavids at the Battle
of Gulnabad and proceeded to lay siege on the capital Isfahan.
Meanwhile, the Russians invaded the northern Persian
provinces, and the Ottomans the western ones. After a brief

resurgence under Nader Shah, which ended with his assassination in 1747 A.D., Karim Khan of the Zand Dynasty ended the 250 year rule of the Safavids. It is likely that the monetary mismanagement, hurting all sectors of the economy, significantly contributed to the fall.

18. The City of a Thousand Mints

Having visited both Anatolia, Persia and the dominions of the Golden Horde and Chagatai, Battúta and his company entered India through the roughest road possible: Hindukush:

> *Another reason for our halt was fear of the snow, for on the road is a mountain called Hindúkúsh, which means "Slayer of Indians", because the slave boys and girls who are brought from India die there in large numbers as a result of the extreme snow and the quantity of snow. (Battúta, 1325-1354, p. 178)*

They successfully crossed the mountain range, but were attacked by Afghan brigands which they with arrows caused to flee. Upon reaching India, another attack occurred, this time by "heathen Indians". Simultaneously, reports of their arrival had already been sent to the Sultan of Delhi, who appears to have put in place an ominous surveillance system of sorts:

> When the intelligence officials write to the sultan informing him of those who arrive in his country, he studies the report very minutely. They take the utmost care in this matter, telling him that a certain man has arrived of such-and-such an appearance and dress, and noting the number of his party, slaves and servants and beasts, his behaviour both in action and at rest, and all his doings, omitting no details. (Battúta, 1325-1354, p. 184)

The Sultan, at the time of Ibn Battúta's arrival, was Muhammad bin Tughluq (Prince Fakhr Malik Jauna Khan), a generous but wrathful despot. H.A.R Gibb had the following to say about this Júná:

> In 1321 the throne was occupied by Ghiyáth as-Din Tughlaq, under whom some sort of order was restored and the authority of Delhi extended again into Bengal and the Deccan. His son Júná, the Sultan Muhammad of Ibn Battúta's time, had his father murdered in 1325, and ascending the throne without opposition "occupied it for twenty-six years of human tyranny as atrocious as any on record in the sad annals of human devilry and then died in his bed." (Battúta, 1325-1354, p. 23)

Sultan Muhammad, who according to Battúta was "of all men the fondest of making gifts and of shedding blood", took a liking to him and promptly recruited him to his administration – an act Battúta did not dare to refuse. As Battúta entered within the immense walls of Delhi, he must have been struck by the emptiness of the city – a warning sign of either war or striking mismanagement, if ever there was one. And although war at the time was a regular occurrence, it would soon dawn on Battúta that it was Sultan Muhammad Tughluq that was the chief cause in turning Delhi into a ghost town. The Sultan's empire stretched far and wide over the Indian subcontinent, which proved ever more troublesome for a ruler with his seat in a city in the subcontinent's far north. Additionally, Delhi stood in proximity to unruly Mongol armies. And so Sultan Muhammad had decided to move his capital from Delhi to Daulatabad further south.

Misguided Generosity

A few years before Battúta's arrival, the moving edict had been given to the citizens of Delhi, informing them that they should start packing. There was naturally a general unwillingness to leave a city where families had stayed for generations, but the Sultan's wish was the population's command. Battúta mentioned this order as well, but might to some degree have been fed propaganda by the elements of Delhi opposing the Sultan:

> *One of the gravest charges against the sultan is that of compelling the inhabitants of Delhi to leave the town. The reason for this was that they used to write missives reviling and insulting him, seal them and inscribe them, "By the hand of the Master of the World, none but he may read this." They then threw them into the audience-hall at night, and when the sultan broke the seal he found them full of insults and abuse. He decided to lay Delhi in ruins, and having bought from all the inhabitants their houses and dwellings and paid them the price for them, he commanded them to move to Dawlat Ábád. They refused, and his*

> *herald was sent to proclaim that no person should remain in the city after three nights. (Battúta, 1325-1354, p. 204)*

Whatever the degree of truth to the insults Battúta mentions, it is certain that the forced migrations occurred. The administration distributed free food and other provisions along the long march, but many died anyway, unused to travels in foreign parts of the land. In the end, the Sultan abandoned the disastrous plan and ordered his people back to Delhi, prompting more deaths. The city stood eerily silent; it was the result of what Indian historian Ishwari Prasad way too forgivingly called "misdirected energy".

In order to explain the monetary tinkering this incompetent ruler soon would pursue, a perhaps positive personal trait of the Sultan must be mentioned as well – his generosity. Ibn Battúta, among others, touched on this subject multiple times:

> *Next day we rode to the palace to salute the wazír, who gave me two purses, each containing a thousand silver dinars, saying 'This is for washing your head,' and in addition gave me a robe of fine goathair. A list was made of all my companions, servants, and slave boys, and they were divided into four categories; those in the first category each received two hundred dinars, in the second a hundred and fifty, the third a hundred, and the fourth sixty-five. There were about forty of them, and the total sum given to them was four thousand odd dinars. (Battúta, 1325-1354, p. 206)*

This well-known generosity was however, according to Battúta, quickly exploited in a comical fashion by a budding sector of opportunists:

> *Every person proceeding to the court of this king [Sultan Mahammad Shâh] must needs have a gift ready to present to him, in order to gain his favour. The sultan requites him for it by a gift many times its value. When his subjects grew accustomed to this practice, the merchants in Sind and India began to furnish each newcomer with thousands of dinars as a loan, and to supply him with whatever he might desire to offer as a gift or to use on his own behalf, such as riding animals, camels, and goods. They place both their money and their persons at his service, and stand before him like attendants. When he reaches the sultan, he receives a magnificent gift from him and pays off his debt to them. This trade of theirs is a flourishing one and brings in vast profits. (Battúta, 1325-1354, pp. 184-185)*

Ishwari Prasad corroborates on this practice:

> *The Sultan's acts of munificence surpass all belief. Whoever went to pay his respects to him carried with him presents, and since the Sultan gave rich rewards in return, the practice became very common. A separate department of presents was maintained. (Prasad, 1933, p. 311)*

It may have been the generous inclination of the Sultan, the above financial and administrative mismanagement, and also a famine that hit Delhi at around this time (likely a result of his exorbitant taxation in the Doab), that caused the Sultan to conduct a disastrous monetary experiment that would prove Gresham's Law true to the fullest extent.

A Tinkering Genius

The Sultan, like so many others, did not properly understand money. What he likely perceived as a lack of silver- and gold coins in circulation – a problem in need of urgent remedy – was likely just people saving and transacting only when there were goods, services or investments that they needed, wanted or found profitable. To remedy this non-problem, and possibly in an attempt to fill the treasury again after bad decisions taken earlier, the Sultan issued a token currency of brass and copper. Ishwari Prasad described the plan:

> *Muhammad Tughluq has rightly been called the prince of moneyers. […] He wished to augment his resources in order to carry into effect his grandiose plans of conquest and administrative reform, which appealed so powerfully to his ambitious nature. There was another reason: the Sultan was a man of genius who delighted in originality and loved experimentation. With the examples of the Chinese and Persian rulers before him, he decided to try the experiment without the slightest intention of defrauding or cheating his subjects, as is borne out by the inscriptions on his coins. Copper coins were introduced and made legal tender; but the state failed to make the issue of the new coins a monopoly of its own. The result was, as the contemporary chronicler points out in right orthodox fashion, that the house of every Hindu – of course as an orthodox Muslim he condones the offences of his co-religionists – was turned into a mint and the Hindus of the various provinces manufactured lakhs and crores of coins. (Prasad, 1933, pp. 304-306)*

Why exactly would households suddenly have incentives to produce identical replicas of these copper tokens? The Sultan had assigned a face value of his new money, at par with earlier coins of pure silver. In the Sultan's mind, it is likely that he thought that by equating the copper tokens to silver by law, and by minting many of these new tokens, more money would indeed circulate in fruitful commerce. The inhabitants of Delhi, however, could produce more of the copper tokens, pay taxes with them as if they were silver, and spend on further luxury articles. Prasad continues:

> The village headmen, merchants, and landowners suppressed their gold and silver, and forged copper coins in abundance, and cleared their liabilities with them. The result was that the state lost heavily, while private individuals made enormous profits. The state was constantly defrauded, for it was impossible to distinguish private forgeries from coins issued in the royal mint. Gold and silver became scarce; trade came to a standstill, and all business was paralysed. Great confusion prevailed; merchants refused to accept the new coins which became as 'valueless as pebbles or potsherds'. (Prasad, 1933, p. 307)

Henry Yule, the translator of Marco Polo's travels, mentioned this event as well:

> The Sultan, in hopes of reviving the credit of his currency, ordered that every one bringing copper tokens to the Treasury should have them cashed in gold or silver. "The people who in despair had flung aside their copper coins like stones and bricks in their houses, all rushed to the Treasury and exchanged them for gold and silver. In this way the Treasury soon became empty, but

170

*the copper coins had as little circulation as ever,
and a very grievous blow was given to the State.
(Polo, The Book of Ser Marco Polo, the Venetian
Vol I, 1271-1295, p. 384)*

Prasad idiotically attributed the utter failure of the Sultan's experiment, not to the Sultan himself but to the Indian people who viewed copper tokens as just that, "[…] however benevolent the intentions of the Sultan". As for Battúta, he remained in Delhi for years, until finally obtaining permission to leave for another pilgrimage to Mecca. That permission was quickly withdrawn however, and the Sultan instead ordered Battúta to accept the position as ambassador to China, which was just as well since the Sultan's Turkish Empire was about to enter a period of revolts, hunger and decline.

The above fiscal disaster is a clear example of Gresham's Law, which states that if two or more monies by law have their nominal value fixed in relation to each other, the good, undervalued (in this case silver) is driven out of circulation while the bad, overvalued is quickly spent. It is also a good example of how monetary tampering, however benevolent and educated the tinkerer, often ends in financial disaster.

19. Chinese Counterfeiters

Leaving Delhi turned out to be as eventful as always for Ibn Battúta. His entourage quickly and by chance became involved in one of the many wars in the area, resulting in some victories but also a very real threat to Battúta's life. During one run-in with Hindu warriors, such chaos ensued that he lost his companions and was taken captive. Sent for execution in the jungle, one of his captors took pity on him and let him go. Battúta, hungry and dehydrated, managed to survive in enemy land mostly by stealing water from basins in villages, and could only after a week relax again and continue his original mission – heading to the Khan of China. On the way, he passed Sultan Muhammad bin Tughluq's Daulatabad and remarked on its enormous size and planning.

Although, as we now know, he at last arrived at a Chinese port and there observed the paper money of that empire, perhaps little did he know of the metallic monies used there before the Song dynasty's lucrative invention. Had he observed the older monies, he would have noticed that it had few similarities with his own Moroccan silver dirhams or gold dinars.

Unruly Beginnings

The destructive monetary system of the 14th century Mongol rule of China was not random, and not only connected to a long-running streak of authoritarianism in the area. It was in fact, in some ways a faulty "solution" to another long-running problem: counterfeiting, which Alison Hingston-Quiggin has detailed in her work. Ancient China, after emerging from monetary darkness into monetary systems of cowries, salt, cloths and tea, can indeed be said to later have evolved into an empire of counterfeiters.

It has already been established that etymology supports the presumption of old seashell money in China, as the symbols for "seashell creatures" and later also for "money" were remarkably similar (Quiggin, 1949, p. 225). Multiple historical documents point to the use of seashell money as well (Einzig, 1949, p. 255). It should then come as no surprise to learn that copper- and bronze imitations of seashells in the 6th and 7th century B.C. perhaps functioned as money as well, just as their metallic oxen counterparts had done in Ancient Greece. Hingston-Quiggin hesitates to call them money as they could have been charms of some sort, but it fits remarkably well with evidence emerging from other civilizations. What was certainly money, however, were the bronze and copper tools used in these agrarian societies, which is why metallic token versions of such items later emerged as money as well.

It is also established that not until the 3rd or 2nd century B.C. were cowries slowly phased out in favor of metallic coinage (which to a varying degree had been in place in the Chinese provinces for centuries). The coins themselves very rarely portrayed the current emperor or king, since it was deemed beneath the rulers to ever let filthy peasant hands touch such depictions. This has made it incredibly hard for numismatists to pair certain coin issues with specific rulers. In any case, round copper coins with central, square holes were minted and functioned for a while as money in parallel with seashells. Due to widespread debasements, the thin coins of the Chou dynasty became so light as to float on water (Quiggin, 1949, p. 243). This triggered a harsh reaction from the first Emperor of China:

> A new era starts with the triumph of Ch'éng Wang of Ch'in, 'the Napoleon of China', who took the name of Shih Huang Ti, the first sublime Emperor in 221 B.C. Much of the uncertainty of earlier Chinese history is due to him, as, in his desire for progress, he determined to break all links with the past. He destroyed the old books, instituting a new script; he abolished the earlier forms of currency (cowries and (?) tortoiseshell, silk and grain, spade-, pu- and knife- as well as roundcoins are mentioned) and issued a new coinage. His dynasty, founded for 10,000 years, lasted 15 […]. (Quiggin, 1949, pp. 243-244)

His copper coins, while surviving a century or so, became debased, adulterated and shrunken in size, weight and value.

Unwavering Production

To the Qin and Han period, Chinese historians attribute the inevitable birth of wide-spread forgery. Emperor Wu Ti (140-86 B.C.), issued silver and tin coins. The largest one was worth 3 000 "pieces of money", but did not circulate even for a year due to private- as well as state forgers (Quiggin, 1949, pp. 229-230). As Chinese coinage largely consisted of copper, any house with a capable smith could issue replicas despite various edicts against such practices. Notwithstanding harsh punishments, 100 000 forgers were discovered in one year alone, resulting in issues being withdrawn a re-cast, with accompanying confusion among merchants and other subjects. Hingston-Quiggin has one source on the subject of near uncountable mints:

174

> *In England there is something infinitely
> respectable about the word mint. It is otherwise in
> China. In the civil wars of that country the first
> sign that a protagonist has arrived (though not
> necessarily to stay) is his acquisition or
> construction of a mint, and also, if possible, an
> arsenal, but the mint is much the more important
> of the two (Fleming, 1936, pp. 301-2). It is not
> surprising, therefore, that the total number of
> Chinese issues is reckoned at some 10,000.
> (Quiggin, 1949, p. 231)*

The return to crude barter in cloths was not unheard of in some areas. One king ordered the reversal of the monetary system to grain- and silk money, only to find that the acts of forgery followed suit, putting moist grain in grain bags, and weaving thin and fleecy silk not made for actual use. The Government of Emperor Yuan (48-32 B.C.) was close to giving up the metal-based monetary system altogether as well, and almost ordered a full reversal to grain, silk, cloth and cowry money. Yet another similar edict was actually implemented by Wang Mang the Usurper in 10 A.D., which threw the economy into chaos after it banned all monies except cowries and various knife-monies – both which had not been in use for hundreds of years. At the time he was murdered, the people had reverted to barter. (Quiggin, 1949, p. 245)

The forgery impetus to later, disastrous paper money experiments may be considered well represented by Qin dynasty emperor Shih Huang Ti, who had banned the use of many primitive monies in 221 B.C. As the copper money had been utterly debased during continuous wars, he decided to issue what may have been the world's first bank notes. Since he knew that making such notes from leather would incentivize the forgers to simply copy the scheme from their own leather sources, he had his own extremely rare and beautiful white stag put aside for the purpose. Each bank note made out of its skin was assigned an arbitrary value of 400 000 copper coins. Though of course harder to counterfeit – and individuals would surely find a way over time – the low number of notes made the money insignificant, if not innovative, in the end. (Quiggin, 1949, p. 248)

Did the copper monetary systems of China have any advantage at all? An Arab merchant operating in China in the 9th century A.D., noted one curious benefit of such coins. A thief breaking into the house of any merchant that only dealt with copper, could very well not escape with all the burdensome wealth the merchant had accrued. This relationship did not hold true for houses containing silver or gold. Although perhaps an advantage for the individual storing his copper money, the low value per weight unit obviously hurt commerce due to transportation costs. But the Chinese stubbornly held true to their copper, knowing full well that hidden dilution awaited the money if cast in silver or gold. It is not clear exactly how widespread various assessment techniques and technologies were in Ancient China, and how that influenced the decision to stick to copper. It is likely, however, that as soon as the cost to assess silver- or gold content of coins decreased, it would increase the opportunity costs of using abundant copper as a medium of exchange.

The widespread forgery, and dilution, naturally hurt the saleableness of Chinese copper money. Copper is, after all, rather abundant in nature, and so forgery may be considered an inevitability. The recurring regressions to barter had often to do with decreases in saleableness stemming from harsh laws passed by kings and emperors, but it is clear that what the authorities termed "forgery", which is just competitive money production, would have had the copper money dethroned naturally as well.

20. The Real Spanish Price Revolution

As we know by now, Ibn Battúta ultimately came back home, where he prepared to head out on his last journey south through the Saharan Desert. China had impressed him greatly, but upon reaching Maghreb (The West) again, he couldn't resist praising the many good characteristics of that land. His short detour to Granada had ultimately proved unsuccessful, which can also be said for the *jihad* as a whole. Castile, later Spain, took hold of the peninsula in the end, and expanded westward while fleeing Moors left both cultural and etymological remnants behind. One such remnant was the *maravedí*, stemming from the Almoravid rulers of Muslim Spain during the 12th century. While initially a gold dinar, the *maravedí* later evolved into a unit of account of Spanish coinage which lasted to the 19th century.

Habsburg Wars

A period where many nations experienced monetary inflation, while operating mostly on gold and silver, was the 16th century. Spain, having reached the New World in 1492 A.D., could finally reap significant rewards from this military investment in the West: large scale confiscation and production of precious metals. This new silver and gold found its way back to Europe through the ports of Seville, Cadiz and Lisbon, from where the flow continued towards neighboring nations. In a sensational wording, this event has been termed "The Price Revolution", or "The Spanish Price Revolution", to emphasize what has been portrayed as a drastic increase in the prices of goods in Europe. Upon closer scrutiny, it appears no such "revolution" in prices occurred; nominal prices in Europe rose with an average of less than 2% per year (Fisher, 1989, p. 895).

The real loss in purchasing power for most Spaniards instead came later, and was knowingly and purposefully imposed on the poorer segments of the populace, not by the market, but by Spanish authorities. The ultimate end-point of such actions resulted in a farcical situation where not even King Philip IV of Spain himself could conjure up enough respect for his Castilian copper coins for them to be acceptable for commerce elsewhere in his kingdom. Akira Motomura, in *The Best and Worst of Currencies: Seigniorage and Currency Policy in Spain, 1597-1650*, discusses related causes and effects.

One of the main reasons central authorities embarked on an armada of debasements was, as we can guess by now, war. In fact, the whole 16th century consisted of Spanish involvement in various conflicts since the empire's dominions stretched as far as the Low Countries, Burgundy, The Holy Roman Empire, Italy, Mexico and Peru. The Habsburg Charles V, who inherited all this and fought to secure it, had to divide the empire as he abdicated to his son, Philip II, who still remained in possession of much territory. Both Philip II and his successors Philip III and Philip IV were involved in wars with France, the Dutch, England, and the Ottoman Empire. Defaulting on debt obligations became a regular occurrence.

Debasements, being a tax not always easily noticeable – especially in times of war when trade and production were disrupted by enemy troops and ships – became a useful tool for these Habsburg monarchs. But since the empire's gold *escudos* and silver *reals*, both above a 90% purity, were much used in international commerce, there was a general unwillingness to tinker with them if not strictly necessary. Instead, focus turned to the billon coinage, consisting of an alloy of majority copper and minority silver, and measured in the unit of account, *maravedís*. Starting at the very end of the 16th century, and continuing long into the 17th century, the slight silver content in billon coinage was withdrawn, meaning it now consisted only of copper. At the same time, the Spanish state increased the *maravedí* face value of the new copper coins, meaning seigniorage rates at the Castilian mints quickly went from below 10%, to 70% (Motomura, 1994, p. 108). Seigniorage rates for silver and gold coins stayed between 1-3% – any higher number and silver- and gold bullion from the Americas would have found their way, legally or illegally, to cheaper foreign mints instead.

Regional 'Monopolies'

Philip IV tried to devalue the silver *real* which had stayed the same in size and content for centuries. The attempt seems to have been a trick related to its weight rather than silver content, as the number of *reales* per marc (which was a weight unit) increased. In other words, it appears Philip IV wanted to decrease the weight of the new *reales*, while still keeping their *maravedí* face value. He quickly reversed his decision however:

> [He] recognized his error and reversed the
> devaluation the following March 12, announcing

> that *"the little utility, and the anger of our subjects and vassals at doing business with this growth [in the nominal value of reales] have been recognized..."* The monarch thus returned to its long-standing policy of silver currency stability. (Motomura, 1994, p. 114)

The King's naughty attempt was more an exception than a rule. The Spanish monetary discipline, when it came to gold and silver, was high according to historian Antonio Domínguez Ortiz:

> *[...] the Spanish Administration's preoccupation with maintaining intact its silver money's credit, even when urgent needs obliged it to continuously alter the billion money; ... [and] show[ed] that considered as a fiscal judgement, undoubtedly very painful, the Administration nevertheless wanted to maintain a solid monetary master for major commerce and foreign goods.* (Motomura, 1994, p. 117)

With copper, or what Domínguez Ortiz still termed "billion" despite a total lack of silver, everything changed. Here is Domínguez Ortiz again:

> *[...] Philip IV understood fully the importance of a healthy currency for a country's economy; if, in spite of that, he consented to such large and lamentable changes in the billion [copper] currency, it was because in the oppression that constantly encircled him he found no other way to get large sums of money quickly... The deflationist effort of 1627, in which he took a direct and personal part, shows that he knew*

perfectly well the gravity of the evil and the
urgency of the remedy. (Motomura, 1994, p. 122)

As has been mentioned already, discipline had indeed shown to be severely lacking when it came to tinkering with the copper coinage. As opposed to silver and gold, copper coins were mainly used in local trade, by local subjects who unlike international merchants could very well not easily resist without the risk of facing threats of state violence. Since the value-to-weight ratio of copper would cause the long transport of such coins to the many mountainous regions of Spain to be uneconomical, it meant that the Spanish mints, and thus the Spanish state, in practice had free reins on such money production. By not having to compete much with mints in neighboring countries, debasing and devaluing copper (first by reducing the silver content, then by changing the face value) became too attractive not to pursue. From having a silver content of 1.39%, that number decreased under Philip II to 0.35% to finance the building of another armada. Philip II's debasement was followed by another one under Philip III, to 0% silver, as part of an offensive against the Netherlands. In 1601 A.D., one marc of copper coins was worth 140 *maravedí*. With the stroke of a pen, Philip III set one marc of copper coins to 280 *maravedí*, meaning he doubled the face value of the new issues, which weighted the same as the old. For the same amount of copper production and import, in other words, the state had suddenly doubled its revenue on its minting of copper coins.

Even higher than the seigniorage related to the striking of new copper coins was the one related to the restamping of old ones – something the state sometimes ordered. Coins minted in 1599-1602 A.D. were ordered for restamping, and the seigniorage rate reached 91% (Motomura, 1994, p. 118). How can we explain this high seigniorage? By ordering the restamping of, for example, copper coins of a face value of one *maravedí* each, the state could gather four such coins from a peasant, restamp them into four new coins of a face value of four *maravedís* each, and subsequently give one of those back to the peasant while keeping the other three. The state could then spend its new copper coins on goods and services not yet adjusted for inflation.

Aside from causing trust in the (copper) monetary system to deteriorate, the Spanish state's policies caused other more unexpected results as well. As subjects received some compensation for the transportation of their old copper coins to the mints, many chose to travel far longer than necessary, which of course meant huge inefficiencies for the economy. A portion of Spain's population, in other words, was paid to walk the country's dusty roads, instead of concentrating on production (Motomura, 1994, p. 118). It is safe to say that, while the copper money devaluations were showering the Spanish state (and military) with short-term profits, the practice very likely had many bad predictable and unpredictable consequences. State contractors, receiving pay in devalued coinage, may very well have left for more honest trading partners. Soldiers, perhaps paid in debased copper coins, may very well have deserted their posts in search of better paid mercenary work. Spain's decline as an Empire was likely not related to the influx of American silver and gold, but from high taxes, continuous copper devaluations, and a bloated bureaucracy.

Finally, in a rather perverse cycle of irony, much of the copper used to defraud the Spanish population in order to finance a Habsburg troop buildup in Austria, was supplied by the Swedish royal monopoly on copper, meaning the Swedes then dying in the Thirty Years' War not long thereafter had supplied much of the means to such an end. We will end the chapters on debasements and tinkering on that note – an evil circle of states profiting and subjects dying. In 1641 A.D alone, in the middle of horrendous war, the mints in Castile minted almost 12 million *ducats* of petty coins, of which more than 11 million *ducats* was seigniorage (Motomura, 1994, p. 119).

A Throne of Gold...

We arrive at the end of the journey once more, having traversed many harsh monetary roads. As 1353 A.D. also came to an end, Battúta and his caravan reached Morocco from the south after having endured other difficulties:

> *I set out thence on the second of Dhu'l-hijja [29th December], at a time of intense cold, and snow fell very heavily on the way. I have in my life seen bad roads and quantities of snow, at Bukhárá and Samarqand, in Khurásán, and the lands of the Turks, but never have I seen anything worse than the road of Umm Junayba. On the eve of the Festival we reached Dár at-Tama'. I stayed there during the day of the feast and then went on. So I arrived at the royal city of Fa's [Fez], the capital of our master the Commander of the Faithful (may God strengthen him), where I kissed his beneficent hand and was privileged to behold his gracious countenance. [Here] I settled down under the wing of his bounty after long journeying. (Battúta, 1325-1354, p. 339)*

The "Commander of the Faithful" on the throne at that time was the Marinid Abu Inan Faris – the sultan who commissioned Ibn Juzayy to record an account of Ibn Battúta's many years of travel. Gold dinars were minted under his rule, like that of the sultans before him.

This leaves us with one last question to ponder, and which arguably has been explored throughout the whole book: why, out of thousands of alternatives and variants, of all sizes, forms, shapes and contents, did Marinid money consist of pure gold coinage upon Battúta's return? Phrased perhaps slightly differently: why did gold, of all things, independently emerge as money among for example the Aztecs, Ghanaians, Tibetans, Chinese, Japanese and Malayans? The answer, grounded on the very dynamics of *hardness* and *saleableness* that we now ought to understand, is of course gold's exceptional physical properties as well as its state of relative abundance, as accumulated through the millennia, in bullion, coinage and jewelry, combined with its state of relative scarcity in nature. Nothing, given an arbitrary price increase, was harder to dilute than gold, and because of this, individuals with enough luck or foresight to use gold as the medium to facilitate economic exchange in the future, without certainty or promise of redemption in value equivalents, found themselves the most successful of all in this matter. Gold, in other words, was not randomly, collectively or socially constructed as money in these societies; it was rather the other way around. Gold, by being globally scarce, constructed an increased probability of less costly economic exchange for individuals adopting it as money, while the opposite relationship held true for individuals adopting other media as such. Not even the many debasements exercised upon coinage could, as we have seen, hurt its saleableness enough to fully regress that development. Such a regression came later as a result of centralized storage (Ammous, 2018, p. 37), but is outside the scope of this book.

The state of the near absolute saleableness of money, which Carl Menger spoke so eloquently about in the beginning of the book, manifested itself also at the very end of the long and chaotic emergence of global monies. Gold, having claimed the throne without coordinated help, accrued such high valuation per weight unit that it became inconvenient in daily commerce – a phenomenon also discussed in the chapter on Lydian electrum coinage. This left, also without coordinated help, a role for silver (and for some time, copper) to play, which is why silver for a long time was highly saleable and highly valuable as well. The gold-silver ratio, for these pure monetary and commercial reasons, was historically often close to 10, as observed in passing by Henry Yule while referring to Shakespeare's *The Merchant of Venice*. It was when the hopeful prince of Morocco was to choose between three caskets of differing metals in order to win the beautiful Portia in marriage, that he had to contemplate current valuations:

> *Is 't like that lead contains her? 'twere damnation*
>
> *To think so base a thought, it were too gross*
>
> *To rib her cerecloth in the obscure grave,-*
>
> *Or shall I think in silver she's immur'd,*
>
> *Being ten times undervalued to try'd gold?*
>
> *O sinful thought! never so rich a gem*
>
> *Was set in worse than gold.*
>
> *(Shakespeare, 1596-1599, p. 59)*

Medieval travelers sometimes observed gold-silver ratios as low as 5:1[29]. As gold first was tokenized in the form of paper money, and then digitized in more modern times, the ability to transfer the ownership of any amount of gold through a central third party caused silver's monetary role to decline drastically. Lacking gold's hardness, holding silver for monetary reasons made less and less sense due to gold's relative increase in

---

[29] See for example accounts on Polo's visit in what today is Myanmar (Polo, The Book of Ser Marco Polo, the Venetian Vol II, 1271-1295, p. 70).

saleableness. Today the gold-silver ratio is closer to 90, which is fully in line with the monetary theory discussed here.

...occupied by an Emperor

With gold emerging as money, leaving hundreds of primitive monies and other metals dethroned in its wake, we have finally verified that "out of many, one" is indeed a fitting summary both in terms of our understanding of how monies of varying hardness and saleableness interact with each other, and also in terms of how, from the many diverse examples discussed in this book, that very understanding emerges. This understanding is both hopeful and pessimistic, and is captured by Ibn Battúta's very first recorded run-in with money and state, which was mentioned in the book's beginning. The confiscation by the Tunisian authorities, of a dying merchant's hard gold dinars – that is the history and future of money. So while hope lies in the fact that money within a saleableness framework now can be understood, not even the hardest, most saleable money in the world is safe against abuse by the very governments entrusted with preserving its integrity. Thus individuals must keep vigilant, and never stop resisting the state's infringement upon the money, or costs long gone are sure to return in new coercive forms.

As gold reigned, saleableness-related shortcomings, such as an ease of production, declined. Instead rose the debasement of gold coins with silver, of silver coins with copper, the shrinking of large coins into small ones, the cutting of heavy coins into light ones, the plating of base coins into "good" ones, the tinkering of nominal face values into higher ones. For any future money, these constant attacks on the money itself need to be extrapolated and guarded against, whatever medium emerges, or economic exchange regresses into some modern equivalent of glass bead peddling, while ships approach on the horizon.

When Ibn Juzayy finished with his commissioned writings on Ibn Battúta's travels, he ended his transcript with a well-deserved thanks in the form of recognitions worth echoing here:

> *Here ends the narrative which I have abridged from the dictation of the Shaykh Abú 'Abdalláh Muhammad ibn Battúta (may God ennoble him). It is plain to any man of intelligence that this shaykh is the traveller of the age: and if one were to say 'the traveller par excellence of this our Muslim community' he would be guilty of no exaggeration. (Battúta, 1325-1354, p. 339)*

Bibliography

al-Sīrāfī, A. Z., & Sulaymān, a.-t. 1. (9th-10th century). *Ancient accounts of India and China, by two Mohammedan travellers, who went to those parts in the 9th century.* (E. Renaudot, Trans.) London: S. Harding, 1733.

Álvares, F. (1540). *Narrative of the Portuguese embassy to Abyssinia during the years 1520-1527.* (L. S. Alderley, Trans.) London: Printed for the Hakluyt Society.

American Numismatic Society. (2002). Retrieved from http://www.numismatics.org/dpubs/romangeneral/

Ammous, S. (2018). *The Bitcoin Standard – The Decentralized Alternative to Central Banking.* New Jersey: John Wiley & Sons.

Ayalon, D. (1958). The System of Payment in Mamluk Military Society (Concluded). *Jornal of the Economic and Social History of the Orient, 1*(3), 257-296.

Balog, P. (1961). History of the Dirhem in Egypt from the Fāṭimid Conquest until the collapse of the Mamlūk Empire. *Revue Numismatique.*

Battúta, I. (1325-1354). *Travels in Asia and Africa.* (H. Gibb, Trans.) London: Routledge & Kegan Paul Ltd.

Bennett, N. (1970). *Stanley's despatches to the New York herald, 1871-1872, 1874-1877.* Boston: Boston University Press.

Butcher, K. (2015). *Studies in ancient coinage in honor of Andrew Burnett.* London: SPINK.

Cassius, D. (A.D. 164–229). *Dio's Roman History* (Vol. IX). (E. Cary, Trans.) London: William Heinemann Ltd.

Chardin, J. (1686). *The travels of Sir John Chardin into Persia and the East Indies: the first volume, containing the author's voyage from Paris to Ispahan.* Westminster: Printed for Moses Pitt.

Churchill, A. (1744). *A Collection of Voyages and Travels, Some Now first Printed from Original Manuscripts, others Now first Published in English, Vol.V.* London: Printed by assignment from Messrs. Churchill, for H. Lintot and John Osborn.

Crump, C. G., & Hughes, A. (1895, March). The English Currency Under Edward I. *The Economic Journal, 5*(17), 50-67.

Einzig, P. (1949). *Primitive Money: In its Ethnological, Historical and Economic Aspects.* London: Eyre & Spottiswoode.

Fekete, A. E. (1996). Whither Gold? *International Currency Price 1996.*

Finlay, G. (1853). *History of the Byzantine and Greek empires, from DCCXVI to MLVII.* Edinburgh and London: William Blackwood and Sons.

Finlay, G. (1854). *History of the Byzantine and Greek empires, from MLVII to MCCCCLIII.* Edinburgh and London: William Blackwood and Sons.

Fisher, D. (1989, December). The Price Revolution: A Monetary Interpretation. *The Journal of Economic History, 49*(4), 883-902.

Foran, J. (1992, May). The Long Fall of the Safavid Dynasty: Moving beyond the Standard Views. *International Journal of Middle East Studies, 24*(2), 281-304.

Garenne-Marot, L. (2009). 'Fils à double tête' and Copper-based Ingots: Copper Money-objects at the Time of the Sahelian Empires of Ancient Ghana and Mali. *British Museum Research Publication 171.*

Gerber, H. (1982). The Monetary System of the Ottoman Empire. *Journal of the Economic and Social History of the Orient, 25*(3), 308-324.

Gold, B. K. (2012). *A Companion to Roman Love Elegy.* John Wiley & Sons.

Grant, M. (1952, June). Roman Coins as Propaganda. *Archaeology,* *V*(2), 79-85.

Gruca-Macaulay, A. (2016). *Lydia as a Rhetorical Construct in Acts.* Atlanta: SBL Press.

Herodotus. (440 B.C.). *Herodotus* (Vol. I). (W. Beloe, Trans.) London: Henry Colburn and Richard Bently.

Hore, E. (1883). 'On the Twelve Tribes of Tanganyika'. *Journal Of The Anthropological Institute Of Great Britain And Ireland,* *12*, 9.

Hughes, A., Crump, C. G., & Johnson, C. (1897). The Debasement of the Coinage Under Edward III. *The Economic Journal,* *7*(26), 185-198.

Kaplanis, C. (2003, September). The Debasement of the "Dollar of the Middle Ages". *The Journal of Economic History, 63*(3), 768-801.

Kaufman, B. (2019, December 30). Retrieved from Medium: https://medium.com/@ben_kaufman/bending-bitcoin-the-principle-of-hard-money-ad577bdfbc14

Keynes, J. M. (1924). *A Tract of Monetary Reform.* London: MacMillan and Co., Ltd.

Kloss, C. B. (1903). *In the Andamans and Nicobars.* London: John Murray.

Liberato, C. (2009). Money, Cloth-Currency, Monopoly, and Slave Trade in the Rivers of Guiné and the Cape Verde Islands, 1755-1777. *British Museum Research Publication 171.*

Malanima, P. (2009). *Pre-Modern European Economy: One Thousand Years (10th-19th Centuries).* Leiden & Boston: BRILL.

Matthee, R. (2011). *Persia in Crisis: Safavid Decline and the Fall of Isfahan.* London; New York: I.B.Tauris & Co. Ltd.

Menger, C. (1871). *Principles of Economics.* (J. Dingwall, & B. F. Hoselitz, Trans.) Auburn: Ludwig von Mises Institute.

Menger, C. (1892). *On the Origins of Money.* (C. Foley, Trans.) Auburn: Ludwig Von Mises Institute.

Mises, L. v. (1949). *Human Action.* Auburn: Ludwig von Mises Institute.

Motomura, A. (1994, Mars). The Best and Worst of Currencies: Seigniorage and Currency Policy in Spain, 1597-1650. *The Journal of Economic History, 54*(1), 104-127.

Onge, P. S. (2017). How Paper Money Led to the Mongol Conquest: Money and the Collapse of Song China. *The Independent Review, 22*(2), 223-243.

Pallaver, K. (2009). 'A recognized currency in beads'. Glass Beads as Money in 19th-Century East Africa: the Central Caravan Road. *British Museum Research Publication 171.*

Pamuk, Ş. (2001, February). The Price Revolution in the Ottoman Empire Reconsidered. *International Journal of Middle East Studies, 33*(1), 69-89.

Polo, M. (1271-1295). *The Book of Ser Marco Polo, the Venetian Vol I.* (H. Yule, Trans.) London: John Murray.

Polo, M. (1271-1295). *The Book of Ser Marco Polo, the Venetian Vol II.* (H. Yule, Trans.) London: John Murray.

Prasad, I. (1933). *History of Medieval India.* Allahabad: The Indian Press Ltd.

Pyrard, F. (1619). *The Voyage of Francois Pyrard Vol I.* (A. Gray, Trans.) London: The Hakluyt Society.

Quiggin, A. H. (1949). *A Survey of Primitive Money: The Beginnings of Currency.* London: Methuen & Co. Ltd.

Rigby, C. (1878). Mr J.M. Hildebrandt on his Travels in East Africa. *Proceedings Of The Royal Geographical Society Of London*(22), 452.

Rolnick, A. J., Velde, F. R., & Weber, W. E. (1996, December). The Debasement Puzzle: An Essay on Medieval Monetary History. *The Journal of Economic History, 56*(4), 789-808.

Roth, H. (1896). *Natives Of Sarawak And British North Borneo Vol.2.* London: Truslove and Hanson.

Schwartz, S. B. (2004). *Tropical Babylons: Sugar and the Making of the Atlantic World, 1450-1680.* University of North Carolina Press.

Shakespeare, W. (1596-1599). *The Merchant Of Venice.* (J. R. Brown, Ed.) London: Methuen & Co. Ltd.

Singer, I. (1902). *The Jewish Encyclopedia: a descriptive record of the history, religion, literature, and customs of the Jewish people from the earliest times to the present day* (Vol. II). New York; London: Funk and Wagnalls Company.

Stanley, H. M. (1890). *How I Found Livingstone: Travels, Adventures, and Discoveries in Central Africa.* London: Sampson Low, Marston, Searle & Rivington.

Sussman, N. (1993, March). Debasements, Royal Revenues, and Inflation in France During the Hundred Years' War, 1415-1422. *The Journal of Economic History, 53*(1), 44-70.

Sykes, P. (1936). *The Quest for Cathay.* London: A. and C. Black.

Tavernier, J.-B. (1678). *The Six Voyages of John Baptista Tavernier* (Vol. 2). (J. P., Trans.) London: Printed for R. L. and M. P. and are to be sold by John Stakey.

Tezcan, B. (2009). The Ottoman Monetary Crisis of 1585 Revisited. *Journal of the Economic and Social History of the Orient, 52*(3), 460-504.

Thomson, J. (1881). *To the Central African Lakes and Back: The Narrative of the Royal Geographical Society's East Central African Expedition, 1878-1880.* London: Sampson Low, Marston, Searle & Rivington.

Wallace, R. W. (1987, July). The Origin of Electrum Coinage. *American Journal of Archaeology, 91*(3), 385-397.

Whitehead, G. (1914). *In The Nicobar Islands.* London: Seeley, Service & Co. Limited.

Printed in Great Britain
by Amazon